To Be A Farmer's Boy

Richard Shaw

AuthorHouse™ UK Ltd.
500 Avebury Boulevard
Central Milton Keynes, MK9 2BE
www.authorhouse.co.uk
Phone: 08001974150

©2011 Richard Shaw. All rights reserved.

No part of this book may be reproduced, stored in a retrieval system, or transmitted by any means without the written permission of the author.

First published by AuthorHouse 25/3/2011

ISBN: 978-1-4567-7628-2 (sc)

Any people depicted in stock imagery provided by Thinkstock are models, and such images are being used for illustrative purposes only.
Certain stock imagery © Thinkstock.

This book is printed on acid-free paper.

Because of the dynamic nature of the Internet, any web addresses or links contained in this book may have changed since publication and may no longer be valid. The views expressed in this work are solely those of the author and do not necessarily reflect the views of the publisher, and the publisher hereby disclaims any responsibility for them.

Acknowledgements

My friends and family give me more joy than I can express. This book is for all of them and, if they are able to read it through, they may understand how some of my quirks originated. I thank Ian Brocket especially and Jaqui Guy for their hard work on the illustrations. Also daughters Penny and Belinda and Choir friend David Millar for their encouragement, proof reading and helpful comments

The sun had set behind yon hill
Across the dreary moor,
When weary and lame, a boy there came
Up to a farmer's door.
"Can you tell me wherever there be
One that will me employ?
To plough and sow, to reap and mow,
And be a farmer's boy,
And be a farmer's boy."

===

The farmer's wife cried "Try the lad,
Let him no longer seek"
"Yes, father, do," the daughter cried,
While tears rolled down her cheek.
"For those who would work, it's hard to want,
And wander for employ.
Don't let him go, but let him stay
And be a farmer's boy,
And be a farmer's boy."

===

The farmer's boy grew up a man,
And the good old couple died.
They left the lad the farm they had,
And the daughter for his bride.
Now the lad which was and the farm now has,
Often thinks and smiles with joy,
And will bless the day he came that way
To be a farmer's boy,
To be a farmer's boy.

Old English folk song,
(origin unknown).

Contents

Chapter 1

"The Farm"

My introduction to farming started at a very early age. I was not born on a farm, nor were my parents farming, but the finger of fate, very literally, took a hand in shaping my future in a strange way.

My sister, two years my senior, contracted a very peculiar disease called "pink", anyway that's what I was told it was called. To this day I've never bothered to find out what its real medical name is or was. Its worst side effect was a softening of the bones and, in a moment of agony, or a poor shot at thumb sucking, my sister bit off the end of her index finger! This deformity in later years, made a mockery of her pointing at something but, at the time, was considered to be a very serious matter.

Mother had to make all the major decisions at this stage in my life as Father was away fighting for King and Country in the Royal Navy. Having been a mining engineering artisan he was a dead ringer for the engine rooms of several of His Majesty's Fighting Ships, playing with all that machinery as a Chief E.R.A. (Engine Room Artificer to the uninformed. What kind of a funny word is "Artificer" anyway?). More about him anon. Mother decided that the chances of me contracting my sister's dreadful, more than nail biting, disease was pretty good and so, at the tender age of about eighteen months I was despatched to "The Farm"

"The Farm" was located deep in the heart of the coal mining district of the West Riding of Yorkshire, in a little village called Carlton with Barnsley being the nearest place to buy a pair of boots. My paternal grandfather, a refugee from Wales some time before, had three children, Jack, the oldest and most inconsequential of individuals, whose life was made comfortably miserable by marrying Audrey, a squeaky-voiced, childless matron who seemed to do little or nothing with her life.

Bertha was next, short and fairly dark, whose claim to fame had been winning some competition which gave her a berth on the maiden voyage of the Queen Elizabeth to New York. My father, Charlie, or Chas, also christened Francis and therefore a Frank, was the baby of the family, some six years younger than Bertha who was two years behind Jack.

Grandfather had been a pretty shrewd old fellow. He owned an Off Licence and general dealers shop, situated in the middle of a row of terraced houses, and directly opposite the main entrance to the biggest coal mine in the district. This collection of two up, two downers, called "Willy Row", was directly down wind of the colliery chemical works and the smell of creosote constantly pervaded the air. The local inhabitants swore that this very pleasant smell prevented them from catching colds. They believed in it anyway! Digging coal from the bowels of West Yorkshire was obviously warm and thirsty work as the business prospered. Grandfather became the owner of several of the terraced houses in Willy Row together with various other pieces of property in the neighbouring village.

Some say he was a hard man and had come by all this property from customers defaulting with the payment of their beer and food bills. I believe he had a good eye for business and purchased them as and when they came on the market. All this property was to cause major fights and general family feuds and disagreements in later years on his demise. He died at the age of 86, still had a mane of silver hair, smoked his pipe, seemingly constantly, and had his pint of ale every evening at his dining table while he played patience with an old pack of cards. He read a lot too, sometimes from tiny little books with the aid of a magnifying glass. His wife, Clara, looked the epitome of a grandmother, fairly short and homely, her grey hair tied in a bun, always with an apron around her waist. I used to sit on her knee and she would irritate me by gently, but absentmindedly, pinching the skin of my neck as a form of caress while talking to whoever was there. But could she cook! Her cakes and buns were a treat never to be missed, and her Yorkshire Puddings? Only my mother made better in my opinion.

Now Aunt Bertha, although attractive, was not exactly a raving beauty but had a distinct advantage over several of the local spinsters, a fairly well heeled Daddy! Some ten miles away, give or take, a bachelor of farming stock, Robert Benjamin Richmond, had a predicament which faces many farming families. His family farm was being run by his father and one of his brothers. No room for another son. A farm in Carlton was up for sale but Robert, (Bob) was penniless almost. Easy way out? Marry the money. So, he courted, albeit rather rudely, Bertha, and then by some means or other, managed to get Grandpa to lend him the money to start his own farm. The farm was quite large in those days, about one hundred and fifty acres, mostly grass with some arable land. Robert wanted a bigger farming operation but how to do it?

Luck and a fellow called Adolf Hitler were on his side. Great Britain entered into a war which she really didn't want, but, to keep up appearances and protect the underdogs over the Channel, entered into. The nation's demands for food were suddenly increased by hungry troopers. The reduction of supplies from the "Colonies" by a very active and intimidating German U-boat fleet had led to food rationing and hungry people. Many acres of adjacent woodlands, for ever in the past deemed unsuitable for tilling, were suddenly brought under the plough. The lands were cleared by an army of strapping Land Girls, local misses and "mississes" who, with their strength of arm almost matching their sexual appetites, soon reduced trees to firewood and exposed some of the most horrendous blue clay soil ever to be tackled by a plough. The trick to all this however was that the Government paid for the clearing! Land for nothing, almost anyway. Good crops were grown, impossible though it seemed, on those horrific soils.

So the farm grew and prospered. Most of the revenue was from milk, selling it pint by pint into the two villages. This was all cash business and it doesn't need much stretching of the imagination to realise that the major name of the game was to prevent the Tax Man from receiving his fair and rightful share of the hard earned proceeds. Remember also that very strict food rationing was also in place at the time and people were hungry. But, who was going to count the pigs every week and who could say if this pig or that had died of some strange and mysterious illness like a long slit in the throat when suspended from a beam in the barn by one leg?

Who is able to gauge, to the pint, just how much milk a cow will give each and every day? Change in food, change in temperature, a longer walk to the pasture or just being irritated by a three year old human being is quite sufficient to put any self respecting cow into a tizz with a consequent reduction in milk. How many eggs will a free range hen lay, especially if she lays half of them under a hedge or in the comfort of a cosy nest in the barn? Yes, go on, prove it Mr Tax Man and Mr Ministry of Food man, if you can. Of course, such activities bring problems of their own too.

Like the cellar door that "hasn't been opened for years, we don't even know where the keys are" hiding sides of well salted bacon which could have been detected by an acute hay fever sufferer from five miles if down wind around breakfast time. Egg shells were boiled and fed back to the hens as the essential grit, needed for egg shell strength, was usually imported. They couldn't be thrown into the rubbish midden as somebody may visit the farm and tell all to the rationing authorities. And milk? Usually found its way into an earthenware jug kept in a fly proof safe in the cool larder.

A far greater problem was the secretion of big, white, five pound notes into as many hiding places as could be remembered. The farm house was built in some bygone day when buildings were not the ticky- tacky of today. Walls of Yorkshire granite, some three feet thick, were an ideal place for hollowing out. I have a recollection of spending a very sleepy night, watching through closed eyes, the bottom of a wall cupboard being chiselled out and stuffed with biscuit tins full of you know what. Welsh dressers and display cabinets, full of cups, jugs and other crockery receptacles, were unusable, unless first cleaned out of these cumbersome notes and coins.

I do remember being taken once to the Tax Man's office with a severe caution to "sit and say nowt" at one of Robin's frequent, but by no means regular, interrogation sessions. We always had to dress in our oldest, tattiest and dirtiest work clothes and make sure we had manure, preferably pig manure, on our Wellington boots. This was particularly effective in winter when interrogation sessions were usually cut short as the Tax Man had to decide between freezing with a window open or suffering considerable olfactory discomfort.

We always blamed it on his government issue, one bar, electric heater. I remember Robert once opening the bonnet of the old car he had, outside the Tax Man's office, and covering my hands with grease and grime and being told not to wipe it off until we had left the office. I didn't know what was going on but, like a faithful trooper, followed my captain into the battle area.

After the war, the Labour party was elected to office and shortly thereafter came the deluge of nationalisation measures. The National Coal Board, who had already mined most of West Yorkshire from underneath us, was the next target for Robert. Firstly, their slag heaps, ever growing, were gradually encroaching onto our farm land, a sure cause for compensation, cried Robert, and proceeded to sue them. Taking all the coal out from underneath us caused massive subsidence and cracked the walls of many of the building. Robert stuck them so hard they eventually took the cheapest way out. They bought the farm and leased it back to him. This move opened up other avenues as the adjacent farm was also put out for lease and was snatched up by Robert too. The farming empire was now about four hundred acres, a large operation in those days. So he had Manor Farm and Stud farm.

I can clearly remember the horses. We had sixteen regular men working on the farm in those pre-tractor days and everything had to be done by muscle power of either men or horses or both. My worst memory of the horses was holding onto the lead rein of this enormous Shire horse in the middle of the street while one of the men had popped into the local shop to buy his regular ten Woodbines. I must have been about four years old at the time and weighed probably as much as the horse's shoes did. Having let my attention wander for a second the horse shifted its foot, onto mine! It was agony. Try as I may I couldn't get the horse to lift its foot. Tears must have been streaming down my face by the time the Woodbine buyer came out of the shop. The big toe on my right foot was severely squashed and was starting to swell like a sausage. Still today, sixty five years later I have an indent and knob on the end of that toe. My rescuer said, in typical Yorkshire fashion, "Tha'll be reet lad, skin grows for nowt", threw me into the cart and away we went. The fact that it went septic later and had to be poulticed......

The horse stable was super place to be in. Each of the sixteen horses had it's own stall, with a manger and a wrought iron hay rack fixed to the wall in front of it. Although the top of each door stayed open except in the very worst weather, it was always comfortably warm in there. The horses were tethered by their halters to the front of the stall and, through iron grills, could see their neighbours, but couldn't bite them. The floor was red cobble stones and had to be kept washed and clean all the time. The horses used to stamp their enormous feet, shod with huge horseshoes and shake themselves until every muscle in their mighty bodies trembled. They were always fed the best of everything. Good, soft hay was specially put aside, just for the horses, never to be fed to common old cows or sheep. Oats were rolled for them in the grinding mill upstairs in the corn chamber. They were led, twice a day when not working in winter, to an old enamelled bath tub in the corner of the stable to drink as much as they wanted. While they were drinking, their individual stalls were meticulously cleaned out and fresh straw bedding careful shaken into place. The harness room was next door, huge horse collars hanging from big brackets fixed to the walls. The heavy working saddles, with a metal centre piece to carry the cart chain, were housed on a long pole. Halters and bridles, some with blinkers and others without, were neatly hung up. Each horse had its own place in the stable and its own harness.

Old Jim was the horseman. He virtually lived in the stable and would have horses harnessed up and ready to go to work before the field staff arrived in the morning. In the evening, Jim would brush and comb the horses and would complain that this horse or that had been worked too hard on that day, and, look at the sweat marks on it. He would clean and oil the harness and insist that any loose stitching or riveting was repaired. The horses loved him and he loved them. He was the only person who could catch a frisky horse when they spent summer in the adjacent paddock. The rest of us would chase the horse round and round the paddock, the horse cantering away, kicking its heels in the air, a grin on its face as if to say what a super game this is. The moment Jim walked into the paddock, all the horses congregated around him, all of them wanting to nuzzle him at the same time.

He was a tiny chap, about five foot five, old, wizened, hardly an ounce of fat on him. How he ever managed to throw a heavy working saddle up onto a very big Shire's back was a testimony to his strength and co-ordination. Everybody else always had to lift the horse collars high in to the air to get them over the horses head. The horses lowered their heads for Jim. He had a long pointed face like, a pixie, one side of his mouth was very much lower than the other having had his pipe hanging from it for sixteen hours a day. He didn't say much and when he did, his Yorkshire accent was so broad that many of the locals had trouble understanding him.

On most farms you will find what "townies" call a duck pond. The fact that the ducks used the pond was purely co-incidental. The ponds were built and designed for the horses. After a hard day of pulling their hearts out, each horse was led into the pond where the cold water was vital therapy for its legs and feet. The horses would stand there for as long as they could. Many of the horse ponds were fancy affairs, brick sides and bottoms to them, others, just muddy puddles. Ours was of the latter variety.

I was allowed to lead the horses by their halters to the pond. I would walk down the side of the pond as the horse walked into the water. When Jim did it, he threw the halter rope over the horse's neck and left the horse to fall asleep on its feet in the pond. I once tried to show that I was in charge of the horse and hung onto the lead rope. The horse walked into the water and the lead rope was too short for me to stand on the bank, and the horse to stand where it wanted to. I kept pulling on the rope to keep the horse close to me, near the bank. The horse had other ideas and a tussle arose. It ended with the horse winning; with one flick of its powerful neck it pulled at the rope. I hung on to it and joined the horse in the pond. The water only went up to the horse's knees, round about my neck height.

I now confess to being afraid of these huge beasts. I had only been kicked once by a horse, as a youngster, and that was sore enough for me to treat the rear end of a horse with the greatest of respect for ever more. I had been bitten a couple of times, once bad enough to draw blood and the rest of the bites to produce huge bruises on my tender young skin. My feet had been trodden on several times, I had been nudged and butted about the stalls when feeding them, swished in the eyes by their tails and covered in water from their mouths when taking them to the drinking bath. To add to all this, they were uncomfortable to ride on, with or without a saddle, and it's an awfully long way to fall down from. I still totally dislike, (fear?), horses.

I didn't spend all my time at the farm, although Uncle Bob and Aunt Bertha, being childless, had more or less adopted me for the duration of the war and my sister's prolonged illness. My mother had moved to Harrogate some thirty miles away, chiefly, I think to get away from my paternal grandmother. Granny was an old harridan who ruled the roost from behind. My parents christened me Richard John, my mother liked Richard but Grandma insisted that I was John, and John I therefore was. I remember we lived, for a while, with my mother's sister, Kath, who had two daughters of her own and whose husband was also away fighting for Winston Churchill.

Mother and Kath were the offspring of the manager of one of the coal mines in the area. Archie was fairly comfortably off in those days, played golf regularly in his plus fours and had a motor car and a pipe and went on holiday to Wales every year. His wife, my real Grandmother, had died around the time I was born. He remarried and got two for the price of one as his new wife insisted that her spinster sister had to live with them too. Poor Archie, he was always henpecked I thought, or was that what my mother thought? They lived in a very big house, with a view overlooking the fields on the edge of the village. The house was unique in that it was the only house in this coal mining village that was painted white. He had two Scottie dogs, one black and one white and both of the perishers used to love biting children. As children, we didn't like visiting there. Auntie Edith fussed over us as only a childless, ageing spinster can, we weren't allowed to run around the house, we had to walk or get admonished by Granny, and, the blasted dogs kept biting us. Grandpa Archie's two females had been brought up only to be young ladies with little or no time for small children.

Everybody had to work during the war and mother had a job at Boots, The Chemist, in the dispensary. My sister and I were packed off to a nursery school every morning, complete with our haversacks containing our gas masks, slung round our little necks . How I hated having to put that mask thing on. The stench of rubber made me want to vomit and in subsequent years this dislike never left me. As a teenager, having to visit the dentist who, in those days used gas to put one to sleep, recalled this rubber stench and my hatred of dentists really stemmed from the mask, and the pain, of course. We children had to have a sleep at lunch time and this was also accompanied by a practice session of putting on the gas mask and so I frequently lost my lunch.

I never had to use it for real but suppose the practise routine was good for us, just in case.

We moved out of Kath's house into a ground floor flat of a three storey building further up the road. I have several memories of this residence where we stayed until after the war was over. I have a picture of my sister and I being in the same bed, sick. Mother said later it was Scarlet Fever. We fought like cat and dog most of the time, probably from sheer boredom, being confined to the same bed as we were. I can remember a doctor coming regularly and sticking a plank on my tongue to look down my inflamed throat, an act which is most conducive to vomiting.

I can also remember getting my first very good hiding at about this time. Being on a slope, the back door of the house had a set of steps, probably five or six, from the door to ground level. My mother caught me swinging a cat by its tail over the railing of the steps. It wasn't our cat, I don't think we had one, but she was not pleased about this at all and showed her displeasure with the palm of her hand across my buttocks! I have never swung a cat by its tail since.

One night I was absolutely terrified and excited at the same time watching a vast number of German bombers heading towards Liverpool or Manchester. The noise of their engines made the ground reverberate and, although we couldn't see them clearly, we could see their shapes blotting out the stars above us. Harrogate was very fortunate, in that the only bomb ever dropped was believed to be from a damaged German plane, limping home. The bomb fell through the roof and straight down the lift shaft of the biggest hotel in town without exploding. It was a fairly well kept secret that most of the planning of the RAF raids was done, so I was told, from another hotel in town which had been requisitioned for the duration of the war for this purpose.

Another inconsequential memory of this place was a friend of my parents who lived in Jamaica or Trinidad who used to visit on occasions and always brought us sweets and chocolate. These items were almost impossible to get during the war days, probably why I can remember him so well. Quite what this friend did when he visited I really can't say as we were too busy making ourselves sick on his sweets! He worked on a Tate and Lyle sugar plantation and this must have had some influence on me in later years.

At the end of our little road was a builder's yard owned by a Mr Batchelor. He had a son, John, who was a couple of months older than I was. John used to go with his father to the building yard, probably at his mother's insistence, and we would play and fight around the piles of bricks and stacks of timber. We had a funny relationship in that we did more fighting than playing for some reason. We were fairly evenly matched in size but I had a distinct advantage. My father used to do a bit of boxing in the Navy and every time I arrived home bloodied I was subjected to the next lesson in self defence or how to try to kill your pals. Having learned a new lesson, I went out and deliberately picked another fight with John to try out my latest techniques. In later years, when we were both Boy Scouts, we had one glorious, serious, punch up, on the outskirts of the Auchingellan camp site situated in the Trossack Mountains in Scotland. That was our last fight and, to the delight of my patrol, I was a Patrol Leader by then, I gave him a very good hiding.

Back to 1945 when much to everyone's relief, the war finally ended. Having been born in 1941 I did not consciously know my father who had been away for most of the war with only a few periods of shore leave. I do remember the great excitement in the house when he arrived home. My sister knew who he was but I didn't and, with the innocence of youth, asked of my mother, "Who's that man?"

That comment, although hilarious at the time to mother and sister, probably hurt my father a great deal and could explain some of his attitude towards me over the next few years.

Father had been in the Navy and, in consequence, had been subjected to Navy rules and discipline. He came home to find a sweet little girl and a very recalcitrant son. I was obviously a naughty little beggar and constantly and obstinately bucked the household system and father's idea of discipline. We seemed always to be at war and of course, I never won a single skirmish, never mind a battle. I spent, seemingly, more time in my room after father came home than I had done up to that time. He insisted that the food that was put on my plate was totally finished, with stories about starving children in China or some other far flung place. If I didn't finish it, it was produced in front of me at the next meal. This created such a stubborn and obstinate streak in me that he must have been quite at his wits end to know what to do with me. He had no personal experience to date of raising a family or dealing with kids and could only recall his own youth and how he had been treated by his father. He was not shy to take his belt off to me either. Mother, I know, didn't really go along with this kind of corporal punishment for minor misdemeanours and I always got a lot of love and sympathy from her to the extent that, when food was re-dished up in front of me, she would always take some and either eat it or give it to the dog we had now acquired. I had tried the dog trick and got caught doing it with punishment being meted out even more vigorously for being a cheat. From all the above it sounds as though I was a battered child. Not really, I don't suppose I was any different to most other strong headed and disobedient children. It certainly soured my early relationship with my father though, something that I now see I missed out on in life. We didn't start acting like father and son until I was about seventeen or eighteen. Sad really, in retrospect.

It was possibly because of this relationship plus "what do you do with the kids in the holidays" question, that saw me spend most, or all, of my holiday time back on the farm with Uncle Bob and Aunt Bertha. It was also due to my parents playing their part in the "Baby Boom" of the late Forties. Within two years of father returning from the war, my sister and I were joined by another brother and sister. Their arrival did cause problems. These were "Father's" children as opposed to my elder sister and I who were "Mother's" children. I was by now six years older than my new brother and really, what does a six year old boy want with babies? Father lavished his attention on the two younger siblings, quite natural I suppose, as he could now play a part in looking after them when they were babes-in-arms, something he had been forced to miss out on with my older sister and me. This lack of paternal affection didn't affect my sister as much as it did me, as an eight year old girl loved having two, real, live dolls to play with! So I jumped at every opportunity there was to go to "The Farm".

I also enjoyed going there because I suppose I got all the attention, Bob and Bertha didn't have children of their own. I certainly enjoyed a different relationship to that experienced with my father, and, I was spoiled by them to a degree. But I had to work for it too. The modern expression, "there is no such thing as a free lunch" also applied to breakfast and tea and supper and any other meal or snack I could scrounge. I was expected to work alongside the men, especially during harvest and other busy seasons. And I wanted to as well because I wanted to be a farmer's boy.

Chapter 2

Tractors

I learned how to drive a tractor at a very early age, leading sheaves of corn from the fields. The first tractor I ever drove was a Fordson Standard. Unlike today's tractors, it had the clutch and the brake combined into one pedal down the right hand side of the seat. It had huge mudguards, and the seat, made out of metal and suspended by a curved leaf spring, had a cushion of a sack filled with hay. The mudguard and seat made ready hand holds for me. To get the tractor to stop, I had to put both of my tiny feet on the pedal and push down with my arms, using the seat and mudguard as anchor points. I couldn't reach the gear lever from this position, nor the serrated throttle lever, so one of the men would put it into gear, set the speed of the engine, and then leave me to it.

I had to steer between the rows of corn sheave stooks while the men threw the sheaves onto the trailer behind. A third man was on the trailer stacking the sheaves. When both sides were ready somebody would shout "Right, go on" and I would slowly ease the pressure from my aching arms, which caused the clutch pedal to rise, with me still on it. Although the average forward movement was probably no more than ten yards and the speed, in first gear, perhaps one mile per hour, the steering wheel was manhandled by me as if I was racing round Brand's Hatch circuit which, in my dreams I was! As the day grew on, and they were long

English summer days, my aching body occasionally let me down and, instead of releasing the clutch slowly, it would pop me into the air. The tractor and trailer jerked forward resulting with the man stacking the trailer being thrown about, or even off the trailer. I learned some choice and descriptive expletives plus had my character analyzed by the stacker man, despite my abject apologies.

It was a greater sin to stall the tractor as it was a hand crank paraffin driven job and not easy to re-start when hot. We had our moments of sheer terror too, when I couldn't press the pedal down far enough to activate the built-in brake mechanism. This always seemed to happen on a steep hill with a full load on the trailer and was followed by one of the men having to dice with death by jumping onto the drawbar between the tractor and trailer to rescue the situation. At least it was generally easier for them to have me with them than for them to continually have to get on and off the tractor. I felt I was earning my keep. I also passed my driving test several years later two days after reaching the legal age to drive! I must have learned something.

I spent many hours on that tractor with Robert and the dog. We, the dog and I, both had our places set aside. I sat on the mudguard on a sack cushion and the dog curled up on the back axle on another sack. The dog was always warmer than I was, lying on the warm axle housing. The tractor droned and droned as we went round and round the field, ploughing or harrowing or some other task. It was quite soporific and often I would slide down to join the dog and fall asleep with it. The noise was something else though. Probably my impaired hearing now was caused by the racket that the tractor made and, of course, in subsequent years, sitting, on other tractors, with a noisy exhaust pipe only four feet from my ears. It was very much later that cabs were a standard feature on tractors, complete with ear muffs and a radio.

Some years later, Robert bought his next tractor, a Fordson Major. Again it was a petrol/paraffin model. The engine was started by running it on petrol and then when it got warm, turning the valve to let it run on the much cheaper paraffin. This first Fordson Major was a big brute, especially to a little boy. It was known to us as the "sit up and beg" tractor from the height you were, when on the seat. It had a tall radiator with canvas screens on it which could be raised or lowered according to the outside cooling air temperature. It also had the first model of hydraulics on it. Hydraulics revolutionised farm machinery design. The trouble was that now you had hydraulics, you had to buy a whole new set of implements to go with the tractor, a costly business. The third tractor Robert bought that I can remember as a youngster, was a Farmall International. The gearing on that tractor was so high that in top with plenty of throttle it used to fly at about 30 miles an hour! An exhilarating ride. The problem with it was there was really nowhere to sit as a passenger as the mudguards were just vertical bits of steel. I was banned from riding on it. This tractor had one of the best pulley drives of anything in production at the time. The tractor would drive the threshing machine or the grinding mill all day and all week if necessary without a problem.

Most farmers are very lucky if they manage to get through life without any serious accidents with tractors. When trailers were being hitched, it was a very simple matter to have your muddy boot slip off the clutch with the tractor in reverse gear and somebody standing behind it ready to insert the coupling pin. Or have one side of the implement attached to the hydraulics and trap yourself between the tractor back wheel and the implement. We had one very serious accident on the farm, not with a tractor though, which occurred when I was at senior school. Most powered implements are fitted with a devices called a slip clutches.

If the machine was overloaded or some object went into it and jammed the works, a slip clutch would come into operation and stop that part, or the whole of the implement from working. It didn't stop the drive power from the tractor though, and as soon as the obstruction or blockage had been cleared, the machine would continue to turn.

Robert was baling hay one day, and by good fortune, another man was in the field stacking the bales into heaps. The weather had not been easy and, with the constant turning and tedding of the hay windrow, the material had become rather like a plaited rope of grass, a bit uneven and lumpy too. The baler was a power take off driven pick-up baler. A rotary drum with metal tines on it would turn and draw the hay into the machine. Then a set of sideways moving arms, called packing arms, would push the material into the baling chamber. Inside the chamber, a metal ram would bash into the "bite" of grass that had been pushed in by the packing fingers to create the bale. Any surplus material was cut off by a sharp knife blade, built into the edge of the ram.

Robert had had a very frustrating day as the machine had continually jammed. It kept taking in too much of the plaited and lumpy material which blocked the pick up reel device causing the slip clutch to activate. Time after time, the precious daylight eating and physically tiring procedure had to be followed; stop the machine, jump off the tractor, clear the jammed throat of the chamber, jump on the tractor and start the machine up again, jump off and feed the material in slowly by hand and then finally, remount the tractor and carry on baling. It happened that on one of these jamming occasions, Robert left the machine running and with his Wellington booted foot, kicked the offending material. The slip clutch stopped slipping and, in the blink of an eye, the pick up fingers grabbed at his boot, the stacker arms pulled his foot into the baling chamber and the knife chopped his foot off in one clean blow.

The man moving the bales was, luckily for Robert, close to hand when the accident occurred. He was able to pull Robert out of the machine which had been jammed by the rest of his leg and body, before it could clear itself and take another bite out of him. He was rushed to hospital, bleeding profusely. Luckily, the man with him had some rudimentary knowledge of first aid or else Robert could have bled to death on the spot. Eventually, Robert had to have most of the lower leg amputated as it was very badly mutilated. The surgeon said it would be easier to fit an artificial limb to the stump of the lower leg than to just the foot. Robert survived this accident. He was a very lucky fellow. What price, too, a little first aid knowledge?

One of the most common machinery related accidents in those days on a farm was loose clothing getting wrapped around the power take off shaft, the spinning shaft which transfers rotary power from the

tractor to an implement. You were regaled with stories of farm workers wearing a scarf and the loose end being caught up by the spinning shaft and, at best chocking the man to death, at worst, if that were possible, decapitating him. The same happened with loose overall belts, trouser legs and jackets left to flap open. I tell this story because, even now, silly accidents like these happen, almost every day. Any machinery and especially tractors in the wrong and untrained hands can be lethal weapons. Children are allowed to ride on tractors and trailers and how many fall off under the wheels and are crushed? Despite modern laws prohibiting such unsafe practises and safety devices like protective cabs on tractors and special guards on shafts, farming accidents still happen needlessly.

Please take greater care than we used to and think about some basic first aid training, you could save a life.

Chapter 3

Cows

One of my first recollections of farming life was being soundly kicked by a cow. I cried, and was helped out of the dung channel by a rather unsympathetic and very amused cow man who had been the instigator of the entire episode. I was ordered back under the cow to try again. Covered in cow manure and wet with urine, which was I most concerned about? Being physically bruised, or having my ego flattened and besmirched as, with all the arrogance of a three or four year old, I had bragged about my untried ability to extract milk from a rather reluctant old cow? Probably to shut me up, a real adult's trick, I had been given a bucket and milking stool and told to "Milk that cow". Was this the beginning of a learning curve about cows? I was going to be a farmer!

Please remember that I am going back over sixty years. Things in those days were a far cry from the modern technological farming methods of today. We didn't even have the new fangled electricity but relied on gas and paraffin lamps and coal fired boilers to heat water.

Being in the dairy business and retailing milk, the herd in those days was housed in cattle byres (called mistles in Yorkshire). These buildings were specially designed to make it comfortable for the cattle and as difficult as possible for the workers. The cattle were kept in stalls, a stall holding two beasts, each tied round the neck with a special chain to the dividing stall partition. Each animal had its own trough or manger in front of it. The sleeping area was slightly raised and straw bedding was placed onto this for warmth and comfort. Behind the stalls was the infamous dung channel and at the back of that was a walkway or pavement, also slightly raised.

The cows were milked by hand in the stalls, the milker sitting on a small stool with a stainless steel bucket, specially designed for the job by having half the top covered in, clutched between his knees. This meant you had to be pretty accurate with the stream of milk to get it into the bucket. Milking by hand looks such an easy thing to do when you see it in pictures. You are always shown happy looking cow men wearing white coats and hats with the cow contentedly chewing its cud being delighted to be relieved of this burden it has carried for the past twelve hours.

Let me tell you my version of how it really is. First of all, you have to wash the cow's udder as it has been sleeping and poo-ing all over the place (anywhere except in the dung channel) for the past half a day. On a winter's morning, when you slap cold water onto a delicate part of the cow's anatomy, its first, and quite natural, reaction is to say "Ooch, that's cold". Without the power of speech it generally takes the only alternative way of showing its displeasure which is to kick out at the perpetrator of such torture.

Cows can kick six ways, frontwards, backwards, sideways, upwards, downwards and frequently when irritated. In other words, wherever you stand, which ever way you go, if you upset it, your chances of being kicked are good. When starting to milk a cow it is always wise to state your intention to the cow that you are about to deprive her calf of something you want. This is done, the text books tell us by patting the cow and making soothing noises to her. We used to say "Cush Cush". In reality it's more a case of standing behind her, putting your hand on her rump and telling her you will kick her if she kicks you. Having warned the cow that you are about to come alongside her with your bucket and stool, did you remember to tell her stall mate too? No? Go back into the dung channel as her stall mate got a fright and kicked you from the side you weren't watching. Pick up the bucket from the dung channel, go into the dairy and wash it out and start all over again.

If you are lucky enough to pass this introductory stage, the next act is to put your head into the soft piece between the cow's back leg and its belly. With your head pushed well in there, the cow has a rather difficult task to raise its leg at you. You also have the advantage of sensing the cow is about to kick before she does and can counter such a move by sticking your arm across its leg in good judo fashion.

Another thing you have to contend with is the tail. Remember that in winter, the cow could have spent several months living in its stall. Its tail, hanging from the rear, has a habit of falling into the ubiquitous dung channel while the cow is lying down and having a little doze. The tail tuft hairs collect dung which hardens and becomes a cross between a cat-o'-nine tails and a mace. Cows are clever creatures and know that if they swish their tails with this weight hanging onto it, the chances are it's going to hurt like hell. A cow's tail is an omni-directional, man-seeking weapon extension of the spinal column. It's going to get you wherever you are.

In the movies a cow always has a perfect shaped udder with four equally sized teats each about the size of a pork sausage. Not so once you leave Hollywood! The back two quarters are usually lower than the front quarters and teat size varies from half a chipolata to a Blut-worst. The text book tells you to hold the teat gently in the palm of your hand and express the milk by manipulating the fingers starting with the fore finger and ending with the little finger on each stroke. Fine, but what do you do if you can only get one finger and thumb around the teat? The answer has got to be a gentle pulling and squeezing action. When milking a cow or newly calved heifer like this for the first time, the task is usually, and periodically, interrupted with walks back to the dairy for a clean bucket.

Remember that the bucket will not stand on its own on the floor as the bottom of the bucket has been panel beaten by the cow, or the lass who washes the equipment, so that the bottom of the bucket has become rounded. The bucket therefore has to be held firmly between the knees at all times and whipped away like lightning if a twitch of a leg muscle is sensed or felt through the head, lodged in the cow's belly area. Cows also have a nasty little habit of holding their milk back. This must be a conscious effort on the part of the cow to frustrate the cow man, especially on a cold, Sunday evening when all he wants to do is get finished and take refuge in his chair in front of the fire at home. Talking to the cow or giving her a fat smack in the guts will normally convince her to be a little more co-operative and to let her milk flow freely. Talk about pillage.

When the milking bucket goes flying, Sod's Law says that it is almost full and invariably winds up in the dung channel. I have seen

them in many other places from the trough at the front to the yard outside and even on the rafters.

The worst sin to commit is to allow the cow to put its foot into the bucket. Firstly, the foot takes a lot of getting out and secondly, the milk doesn't usually pass the Ministry hygiene test afterwards. That is one of the reasons why there is always a proliferation of well fed cats in a cow shed and they certainly don't cry over spilt milk.

Cows drink vast quantities of water every day, it can be ten to twelve gallons or more. Now some of this water is converted into milk, say three to four gallons a day. Where does the rest go you might ask? Normally, the cow has a good try at getting it into the milking bucket. Failing this, the splash from the dung channel also tries to get into the bucket unless the alert cow man either covers the top of the bucket with his hat or his hand. A drop or two will go by unnoticed when mixed with several hundred gallons so it was never too much of a concern. However, a wet hat that has to be worn for the rest of the day with the brim almost touching the nose is another matter entirely. Most cowmen I knew used vast amounts of Brylcream on their hair. I was told it acted as a waterproofing agent.

As mentioned earlier, the first time I was ever kicked severely as a small lad, I found my way into the dung channel. I have also been kicked into the trough in front of the cow. It's hard to know who is most startled, you or the cow when this happens. When you get a really bad tempered cow there are several things one can do to overcome its resistance. Having somebody hold its tail vertically in the air does reduce the incidence of kicking. This, if assisted by a pair of bull nose tongs, also held high in the air to keep its head up, will stop the antics of all except a determined man-killing Friesian heifer who has spent summer out on the moorlands. When all these measures fail, send her to the market. There you hope some sucker with more strength and patience than you, buys her.

Have you ever seen a cow man's arms and wrists? Never challenge a cow man to arm wrestling. He could crack Brazil nuts with his fingers after a few years of hand milking. Being constantly exposed to water, milk and other liquids plus the vast amount of manual work done on a farm, the skin on the palms of his hands soon turns into an instrument of torture. His hands become akin to emery cloth. They get even worse in winter, becoming chapped and cracked, and in summer, these chapped areas have to heal up to make room for the blisters, thorns and thistles which are associated with summer harvesting and haymaking.

Now all the above was not learned at the tender age of four. At three you are told by the friendly cow man, whose activities you are interfering with, that the cow he is milking has got a greenfly on the end of its teat and so you get closer to look. The cow man then manages to direct a perfect stream of hot milk straight into your eye, all over your face and shirt. This can, and probably will, start to smell after a couple of hours, especially in summer. Having been caught with the non existent green fly you will not fall for that again but will fall for at least two more wondrous things over the next six months such as a wart or a sixpenny piece stuck to the teat end. "How did this get here?" will be the opening gambit as he examines closely the end of the teat. You can't resist going to look at it.. .

Having mentioned warts, they were fairly common things to find on a teat. The cure for them was to wait until they were big enough and then tie a hair from the cow's tail around the neck of the wart. The wart usually fell of within a couple of days, usually into the milking bucket of course.

As time goes by and you get a little stronger, the next task delegated to you is the cleaning out of the dung channel. Cows eat an extraordinary amount of food. I was first told they had to as they have four stomachs to fill. Eventually this food finds its way through the digestive system and, theoretically, is deposited in neat and tidy piles in the dung channel. Here it is mixed with some straw from the bedding material which has worked its way backwards and becomes a nice little job lot. As with all rules there are exceptions. Cows get bored standing facing the wall like a classroom of naughty school children and so, on occasions, decide to turn as far as their restraining chain will allow and have a look around the place. Depending on the size of the cow and the congeniality of its stall mate, it could actually put its back feet into its stall mate's trough. It is at this moment in time that nature calls urgently and somebody has then to clean out the trough. This is not such a bad task if the incident happened a few hours ago and it's cold and hardening. If it's fresh and a bit runny, it's another matter, one which evokes a constant string of colourful epithets from the cleaner about some animals' unseemly habits. Of course the cow hasn't a clue what you are going on about.

Before dehorning cattle became a common practice it was a dangerous mission, bending in front of something with twelve inches of solid, pointed, calcified matter stuck to its head and taking exception to a) you being there and b), it is pretty cross at not having eaten for hours since the fouling of its food incident happened.

The time of year all cow men dreaded was the change over from winter feeds to fresh summer grass. To avoid the risk of bloat we always let the cattle into the oldest pasture first and for a limited time too. Nevertheless, the change of diet to something a little more laxative created a certain looseness. This became a deadly projectile as, when walking down the pavement behind the cows, one would start its business and then, suddenly, cough. That was a certain complete change of clothes. It also played havoc with the wall paint.

All this precious manure had to be forked, shovelled and brushed into the largest wheelbarrow on the market. The full barrow was then wheeled out into the yard where, after several months of winter, a mountain of gently steaming manure cooked itself into the finest fertilizer in the land. As the midden got bigger there were two ways to get the next barrow load to the top of the heap. You either threw it up with the aid of a muck fork or you put a plank on the heap and took a mighty run at it. Running up a twelve inch plank covered in frost and droppings, pushing a heavy barrow load from the dung channel, is akin to walking the policeman's white line on New Year's Eve. Which ever way you stray you are deep in the manure!

Before breeders started playing with cattle genetics and the like to produce naturally polled, or hornless, animals, horned cattle were a problem of their own. An anxious newly calved heifer was a match for any modern day matador. Getting cows stuck in hedgerows was another occupational risk. Now even hedgerows have disappeared. On occasions, horns were knocked off during some friendly or serious tussle with a rival in the field. The animal would come in looking all lopsided with a bloody mess down its face. I can assure you that there is a mighty monster of a blood vessel serving the horn. In summer such wounds had to be quickly treated to prevent flies from laying their eggs there or face losing a valuable production unit. We were advised by The Ministry men to dehorn all cattle. It was a simple job when calves were born to nip out the horn bud with a special hot iron. When it came to full grown animals it was a different story. The vet said if we used a wire saw, the heat produced would cauterize the wound as it was sawn and it wouldn't bleed. An anaesthetic injection was given at the base of each horn, not an easy operation as holding the cow's head steady was a Herculean task. The wire saw was then applied with considerable vigour. As the horn fell off, the jet of blood squirted over everybody in a three yard radius and the animal shaking its head didn't help matters either. Maybe the vet knew some trick that we hadn't learned about. After a few days the animals looked a lot happier although the milk yield fell dramatically during this time.

Cows are funny social and status conscious animals. They are also creatures of habit. Before we had piped water to drinking bowls in front of each animal we had to go through the daily routine of letting the animals loose, two at a time, to drink from a water trough outside the mistle or cow shed. While they were drinking their bedding was forked over, loosened and fresh bedding straw laid for them. There was also something to lure them back into their stall in the form of sweet

smelling green hay or juicy oat straw. It was fascinating to watch the "senior" cow refuse to allow the junior cow to drink until she had had her fill. The senior cow would then almost trot herself back to her stall where she proceeded to get stuck into her stall mate's half of the hay. She would also do her damnedest to keep the junior cow out of the stall. The experienced cow man would know the greedy one and would chain her up as soon as she entered the stall. Cows became used to their own stall positions and woe betide you if you tried to change their places around. In summer, when the herd was brought back to the mistle for milking, the cow man merely opened the door and shouted "Come on" to the assembled herd. Each cow would sedately walk in and go straight to its habitual place in the stalls and stand waiting to be tied up. When walking between the cows in the stalls, if they were standing at an angle, backside to backside, you simply had to say "come over" and they would move apart to allow you access between them. If you changed a cow's side from left to right and shouted come over, the cow moved in the opposite direction making it impossible to get between them without a pushing contest.

I am certain that cows, and most other animals too, have some form or means of communication, a language which only Dr Doolittle was able to understand. Have you ever watched a herd of cattle in a field suddenly decide it is time to have a drink from the water trough or pond? They don't go one at a time but all go together as if some hidden publican has shouted "Bar's open". Have you noticed that in the heat of the day they will all try to get under the same shade tree at the same time? That's like a bunch of ladies at a Mother's meeting. If one beast found a gap in the fence into the next door field of young corn, it would only be a matter of minutes before almost the entire herd were scoffing away.

I say almost the entire herd because there always seemed to be a few "goody goodies" who would never do such a thing. They were either paragons of bovine virtue or, maybe, were they just too stupid? It would be the same animals who, when called to enter the mistle, would decide to stay in the yard and had to be driven in. Cows also seemed to have their own circle of friends to whom they would stick close while in the pastures, and would groom each other with their tongues. Cows are fairly clean animals and do spend time licking themselves. I was always taught that licking themselves was a sign of good health and, when an animal had been sick, we were always delighted to see it grooming and knew that it was on the mend. Friendly cows could often be seen grooming their pal's forehead, the tuft of hair between the horns and the neck. These are the places that a cow can't do itself of course but how did its pal know that it was time for a wash and brush up? They acted as the best of friends, like two young girls helping each other with their coiffures before a party. It could only have been made possible through the medium of this cow communication channel.

A cow's tongue is a wonderful piece of Mother Nature. It is long, incredibly mobile and rougher than a carpenters rasp. Cows use their tongues almost like a lasso when eating long grass. They wrap their tongues around a tuft of succulent grass and pull. When a cow got to know the cow man it would often give him a lick of affection. When

this happened to me I was usually so filled with pleasure that I hardly could complain about the scouring I got. I once heard a story of a fellow who was "tree'd" by a very irate bull. He lost a Wellington boot on his hasty climb (or jump!) up the tree and couldn't get high enough up the tree to keep his feet out of the way. The bootless foot was his sole (no pun intended) means of support on a low branch of the tree. After going through its snorting and dancing performance the bull settled down to licking his foot and it wasn't long before his sock was gone and the skin off the sole of his foot too! He, of course, couldn't and wouldn't move.

This amazing tongue is housed in an equally amazing mouth. When a calf is born it usually has small "milk" teeth on its bottom jaw and a set of baby molars. A cow in common with all ruminants, never get upper teeth but has an incredibly hard pad of bone or gristle instead. As the animal gets older, so the milk teeth start to be replaced with a bigger, second set, just like human beings. The age of a cow is easily determined by looking in its mouth and counting the number of second teeth. The first pair, growing from the centre, always come out at about the age of twenty one months and, thereafter, the cow gets two more teeth every six months until it has a "full mouth" or eight front teeth at three years and three months old.

Despite the lack of top teeth they can still bite, although rarely do so in anger, and the result is usually a whacking big bruise on one side and teeth marks on the other side of the particular piece of your flesh. Because of this dental arrangement that Mother Nature gave to cattle, they have an awful struggle trying to eat very short grass. They need something they can really get their tongues round. This is one of the reasons why a good farmer would usually have a few sheep to follow behind the cattle in the grazing cycle. Sheep, although they don't have

top teeth either, have smaller mouths and prefer eating half sized grass. Also, because a sheep's legs are shorter than a cow's, their mouths are nearer the ground when eating! So I was told.

Having teeth growing at predetermined and regular times was always a boon to farmers and butchers at the market, where, if you didn't inspect the teeth of a prospective purchase you could wind up with an animal considerably older than you had bargained for. With all the food that cows eat their teeth must take quite a hammering. Having said that, I can't ever remember a cow having toothache! Would we have known if it had anyway?

We had to walk our herd through the village street to get to the pastures and meadows. Normal procedure was to keep the entire herd in the yard until they were all finished milking and then take them down the road at a slow, udder wobbling walk. If the yard gate was inadvertently left open, it was not unusual to see the cows taking themselves down the road to the field. And they usually got to the right field. In those days "road rage" hadn't been invented so traffic was not a problem. Spring gardens without fences or walls were fair game though and many a harsh word had to be taken from keen gardeners, some we were convinced left their gates open on purpose, wanting to claim some form of compensation which, I might add, they never got. I can remember one old pensioner who used to wait until he saw the cows walking down the road and then he would follow behind with his bucket and shovel picking up the droppings for his garden compost heap. Maybe he was the inventor of the modern day "poop scoop" the use of which is demanded by law for dog owners in some countries these days. I bet the modern "poop scoop" owner can't grow chrysanthemums and tomatoes like he could though.

Although the majority of our milk was sold into our village and the neighbouring village, we did wind up with surplus milk, especially in summer. This was sold to the Milk Marketing Board in ten gallon churns. It was collected every morning of the year from a stand built at lorry deck height on the main village road. The stand was a good hundred yards or more from the dairy and the ten gallon churns had to be rolled or carried to the stand.

Churn rolling is an art which requires a great deal of practice before a reasonable level of proficiency is attained. It was not unusual for an amateur to let the churn roll faster than he could cross his hands, which usually resulted in a long, white, telltale stain running down the yard. This also caused the boss to have a severe valve bounce as ten gallons of hard fought for milk oozed its way into the soil or drain. Once at the stand, the churn then had to be thrown up onto the top. Now a full churn of ten gallons, plus the container, weighs about one hundred and twenty five pounds. This was a snatch and jerk lift which many Olympians would be proud of. I can't remember how old I was when I first managed this feat but I remember being extraordinarily cocky and proud the first time I did it. The problem thereafter was that nobody would help me to lift them as they had done previously. Churn rolling races also featured high on the local farmyard amusement list. It was always safer to do it with returning empties though.

Keeping the milk cool in summer was a nightmare without the aid of modern cold rooms and refrigerated bulk tanks. Milk is hot when it comes from a cow. It was cooled in the dairy using a water cooler, a chromed copper contraption made by bending pipes to look like a musician's washboard. Cold water flowed through the pipes and the milk was allowed to dribble slowly from a header tank across the outside of the coils. It then went through a fabric sieve called a "sile", and into the churn. The now warm cooling water was used to fill up the drinking trough outside. In summer we had to cover the churns with wet sacks to keep them cool and, in the day time, with a white sheet on top of the sacks to keep the sun off. I can remember that the last thing we did before going to bed on a hot summer's night was to go to the dairy and slosh more water over the sacks.

Thundery weather was always a cause of concern for two reasons. By some strange circumstance, milk seems to go sour very quickly in thundery weather. I don't know why, but our vet had a theory. The cows were always a little nervous during the summer flash, bang, crash and rattle storms. Let's be honest, who isn't? Sometimes a good storm, right on top of you, can terrify the most hardened soul. The vet reckoned that the fear produced something called adrenalin in the cow which got into the milk and made it go off easily. He was a clever man, our vet.

Milk is also very sensitive stuff and easy to contaminate. The slightest whiff of paraffin, diesel or silage around a dairy and the milk picks up the smell and you can taste the paraffin or diesel or silage as you drink the milk. Now, if you didn't leave the top of the milk churn partially open through the night, the milk would go musty too. So, it was a bit of a poser. Leave the lid on and get musty milk or open the top and hope there was nothing around with a strong, pervasive smell. Although hot weather was a testing time, in winter we had to cover the churns to stop the milk from freezing during the night!

One of my greatest boyhood pleasures was to sneak into the dairy and, using the pint measure with a handle on it, scoop up a pint of the creamy top of the cold milk and drink it. Even today that habit still persists but now I go to the fridge!

Remember that a cow has to have a calf before it will produce milk and so, some three months after it had produced its last calf, the cow was put to the bull again. With a gestation period of nine months, the cow would produce a calf every year at about the same time. Good husbandry dictated that a cow should have a rest before producing her next calf and so we would start to dry off the cow by cutting down any supplementary feeding and only milking it once a day. The cow soon got the message and stopped all milk production for about six weeks before the next calf came along.

I can remember one very good cow called Christel, who, as regular as clockwork, produced her calf on Christmas Day. No such thing as Public Holidays for dairy farmers. She was an easy calver too, used to pop it out in a matter of minutes without much help. Some of them, especially first time heifer calvers, needed quite a lot of assistance. This was a bit of a messy business requiring a calving rope to be attached to the calf's front feet while it was still inside its mother. The strength of a cow's insides have got to be felt to be believed. She could almost break your arm.

The worst scenario was always a breach birth, the calf trying to come out back feet first. This meant a difficult, and not always successful, task at which most cow men were fairly experienced. The calf, trying to get out backward usually got something stuck, a leg or its backside. It then had to be pushed back in again, rolled over, turned around and then the front feet secured with the rope. All this with the cow hopefully remaining on its feet, paddling about all over the place in obvious discomfort. The cow man was also very uncomfortable with his arm, up to his shoulder, pushed into the cow as far as it would go and working purely by feel in the dark confines of the cow's womb. If you study the anatomy of a cow fairly closely you will deduce that the cow man's face during this task is but a few inches away from the cow's defecating organ! All this heaving and straining, pushing and pulling usually resulted in the cow not caring about where her muck went as long as she got rid of it. Yes, you've probably guessed where it usually found its way to! No?

If you have ever seen old pictures or photographs of farm workers in, say, the late 1800's, you will note that they had a piece of string tied around their trousers just above the calf muscle. This, I was told, was to stop rats from running up their trouser legs during threshing of corn. Then some member of the Royal Family, a fellow called the Duke of Wellington, got sick and tired of getting his trousers dirty when fighting for his country in muddy foreign lands. He came up with a brilliant idea and gave his name to a very useful bit of footwear, the Wellington Boot. Such boots were fairly standard farm winter wear and all year round wear for cow men due to the fairly wet nature of their work. Great, until you were standing very close behind a calving cow.

The open tops of Wellington boots are cleverly designed to catch anything that falls from above and, sure as blazes, they did. Now I see some very clever fellow, probably an ex-cow man, redesigned the top of the boot and put a strap or tie string around the top. That's fixed that. Now you only get it down your overalls or apron.

Eventually, after much huffing and puffing, slipping and sliding, getting covered in muck and urine, the calf would come sliding out at such a rate of knots that whoever was pulling on the rope could easily find himself sitting on his backside in the dung channel. But the job is not over yet. Get up! Open the calf's mouth and clear out any mucus, blow into its mouth, take some straw and rub its rib cage.

If it hasn't started breathing, smack its ribs until it does. Push a bit of straw up its nose. That usually causes it to snort which blows all the mucus out. The poor calf, after a difficult birth, was as exhausted as the cow and the men. Mother by now is calling for its calf, remember she is tied up so can't get to it. Drag the calf up to her head and just watch how she licks it clean and dry. We always sprinkled a little salt on the calf so she could lick that off too. Then mother needed at least one if not two buckets of warmish water or oatmeal gruel to drink and she was happy. A few hours later you could go back and see the next wonder of Nature. The calf, on jelly legs, rummaging around the back end of the cow to find nourishment. How do they know where to go and what to do when they get there? Mind you, I have seen calves trying to get something from the front end of a cow for quite some little while before realising the action is taking place elsewhere.

Most older cows accepted man's intervention in this wonderful act of Nature without a problem. Some cows though, on having a calf, would immediately revert to their pre-domesticated days and chase anybody away from her helpless infant. I've seen them go absolutely berserk if they weren't tied up. Sometimes they would have their calves out in the field in summer. All the rest of the herd would stand around and watch like a bunch of learner midwives. I am sure they were making encouraging noises through their communication system. "Come on now, Haybelle, one more big push". Then to get the cow back to the farm yard you had to take a sack, put it over your shoulders to avoid getting wet through, pick up the calf (another good weightlifting exercise), two of it's ankles in each hand and walk with the calf on your shoulders in a fireman's lift. The mother would get quite agitated and follow you, sometimes a little too closely for comfort if she had long horns. Other times it took three people, a horse and cart and a lot of stick and deception to be able to get the calf away from the cow and into the cart. Last man in the cart was usually the matador!

Just like expectant fathers, we wanted to know the sex of a calf almost before it had hit the ground. The female, or heifer calves, were never too much of a problem as the herd always needed replacements so the best progeny were always in great demand. The bull calves were needed by the beef producers and were generally sold to them after weaning. Most dairy farmers did not have the land or resources to keep all the calves their herd produced. As a matter of principle, we never knowingly sold our calves to veal producers. It just didn't feel right somehow and what a waste of future roast beef too.

Herd replacements were also needed because at about this time, there was a national programme to eradicate tuberculosis from cattle and therefore, their milk and meat. The Ministry man would come and give each cow a jab in its neck area. About a week later he would come again and inspect the results. If there was a swelling, the cow was deemed a tuberculosis carrier and was despatched to the knacker's yard. This performance happened at fairly frequent intervals to both the dairy herd and the young stock too. So any surplus TB free animals were in great demand throughout the county.

As well as TB, there was also another nasty disease which took its toll of calves. In those days I don't remember it having been diagnosed as a disease though. The dreaded one was a cow having a premature calf, called "slipping its calf" in local parlance. This was blamed on a variety of things from fresh grass to "that paddock", from the dogs running the cattle, from the cow men chasing the cows through the yards and mistles, in fact, to almost anything at all. It was only many years later that Contagious Abortion or CA came to light. This was always a messy business as the calf carcase had to be disposed of, usually by digging it into the manure midden where it rotted away very quickly or a big hole dug somewhere. The former was the easiest as the ground could be frozen solid for months during winter. It was a sad thing too as the cow concerned never really seemed to recover and was frequently sent to the knacker's yard or, if she looked reasonable, was passed off as a newly calved cow at the market.

Markets and market days were a calendar highlight in those far gone days. They were fascinating places. Cattle bellowing, sheep and lambs bleating away, pigs squealing as only pigs can, gates being clanged shut, drovers shouting and whistling. It was all hustle, bustle and noise. There were always side stalls too. You could buy a good pair of boots, reins and tackle for horses, patent medicines for animals and humans too. Pork pies and steaming cups of tea in thick chipped white mugs with plenty of sugar. Where they got the sugar from was always a mystery as we were a nation on rationing at this time. Hats and caps of all descriptions, raincoats and "Wellies", walking sticks, shepherd's crooks, penknives, milking buckets and stools, new cartwheels, tools, picks, shovels, spades, muck forks, potato forks, root forks, hay forks, galvanised baths and basins, wheelbarrows, anything you wanted. Then there were those fascinating showmen salesmen, the one who demonstrates a set of kitchen knives which will cut anything made on earth right before your eyes. "This set is selling in London for ten shillings, but, I'm not selling for ten shillings, I'm not selling it for eight shilling, I'm not even selling for six shillings. This amazing set is being given away today for ONLY FOUR AND SIXPENCE!!!!!"

We bought a set of "unbreakable" pottery once that the salesman was bouncing all over the trestle table in front of him. We hit a couple of potholes on the way home and wound up with half a set.

Sometimes we went to market to buy, sometimes to sell and sometimes just to see what prices were like. This was easily found out at lunchtime in the local market pub over a pint of ale and a sandwich, (lemonade for me, please.) If we were selling a cow, she was put through the "beauty parlour" before being loaded onto the truck. She was washed and curry combed and the tangles and muck taken off her tail. Her horns and hooves were given a wipe over with linseed oil and my, didn't she look a treat!

To give her udder that fine, full, highly productive super shaped look, she was usually only half milked that morning and her teat ends dipped in collodion to seal the teats and stop the milk from running out. When she got to market the combing and wiping was repeated and we all had to have the same story ready for any prospective buyer; her age, (Do you want to look at her mouth, Mister?), how many calves she had produced, how much milk she could give, her temperament, did she calve easily, had she ever slipped a calf, etc., etc.. Of course nobody ever admitted or owned up to the fact that one or more of these problems was the reason for selling her. The stock answer was that we didn't have enough corn, hay, turnips, straw or whatever, depending on the present season. We didn't exactly tell lies but, we didn't always tell the whole story either! If a good friend was interested he would be told that she was "not your kind of beast" and we would wait for some novice, or an unsuspecting buyer who farmed a long distance away, to come along. After all it was an open auction and let the buyer beware!

In due course the animal would be walked into the sale ring and paraded around for all to see. It was not uncommon for a seller to have a pal in the buying tiers primed and ready to push the bidding up a little. That sometimes backfired when he was left with the final bid on the animal and a lot of talking then had to be done to the previous last bidder to get him to take it. Sometimes that didn't work either and we found ourselves taking her back home again with egg on our faces.

In trying to get these deals to finality, not only was there some footwork to do but some hand work too. The seller would hold, in his left hand, the buyer's right hand, palm up. The seller would ask his

price and slap the buyer's hand with his own right hand. This bit of strange behaviour continued until agreement on the price was reached. On concluding these outside deals, the seller and buyer each used to spit on his own hand and then shake hands on the deal. That shake meant the deal was signed and sealed and woe betide anybody who reneged on his half of the deal. He usually had to travel miles to find a new market. The shaking of hands on a deal is still in place and a good man is as good as his handshake but the spitting on the hand? What happened to that I wonder? Probably banned in the interest of public hygiene.

Beef cattle markets were somewhat different in nature. Many of the buyers were butchers looking for stock to slaughter. In the days before digital, computerised weighing machines and their predecessors made their appearance at every cattle market, it always amazed me how a good butcher would size up the animal's weight by eye, to within a few pounds. After all, he was buying weight of meat remember. After weighing machines were installed the trick was to feed the animal with a bit of salt before it left home and let it drink as much water as it then surely wanted. Water is the cheapest thing to increase weight very rapidly and it always fetched the same price per pound as meat! The butcher would have been around the pens before the sale started, looking each animal over, very thoroughly, beforehand. He would invariably want to see inside the beast's mouth to check its age. He could tell to the ounce by feeling next to the tail, the ribs and the backbone just how much of the animal was meat and how much was fat. He wanted a reasonably fatty animal as in those days what was cholesterol anyway? Beef always cooked better in its own fat and if it was too thin, he would know that it was going to be tough. Remember that roast beef and Yorkshire pudding was a Sunday tried and tested county, if not national, ritual and he didn't want Monday morning to be spoiled by a vociferous Mrs Henshaw complaining that her "'usband Albert said it was the worst bit of meat 'e'd ever 'ad in 'is life". The Mrs 'enshaws were not to be trifled with either as they would blacken your name throughout the village and then every housewife would say "I don't want any of that rubbish you sold Mrs 'enshaw". Today, that's called customer resistance. What can you do now, when all you get is a plastic wrapped bit of meat from a supermarket assistant who has a hard time telling beef from pork if the label has come off? Oh, where are the real butchers of yesteryear?

For all the nonsense one had to put up with, working with cattle, especially dairy cattle, was a very satisfying occupation and life was never dull. A good cow man knew each and every cow by name, who were her dam and sire, how old she was, how many calves she had produced, how much milk she should give at the morning and evening milking. He was concerned if the volume didn't match the expectation as this was usually a sign of something going wrong or impending sickness. These days, most farmers have all this information on a computer! The cow man was at peace with his animals and, more importantly, the cattle were at peace with him. We once had a fantastic cow man called George, who also had a very good singing voice. He would sing as he worked his way through the stalls of cattle. He could

also, much to my great envy, yodel. One song I remember him singing often with a yodel in it was the Irish tune "I will take you home Kathleen". Many years later, some smart University trained fellow advocated playing a radio to improve milk yields. What was wrong with George might I ask? When he took his annual two weeks at Scarborough or Bridlington, we could see the difference in the number of milk churns on the stand.

Despite modern technology, milk production is still a daily fight against the weather and the economics of the day. Dairy farmers were, and still are, very rarely the richest farmers in the land. The big advantage to retail milk was that we got the money straight away, or at least at the end of the week. From the Marketing Board you could rely on a cheque at the end of every month and that kept the bank manager happy too.

We had a retail milk round. The milk was decanted into bottles which had been specially printed with the farm name on it. There were pint bottles, two pint or quart bottles, half pints and a third of a pint bottle, called a gill. There were twenty pint bottles to a crate, a solid, heavy, galvanised wire affair, specially designed to make the bottles rattle in a very irritating fashion. The bottles were laboriously washed by a lass in the dairy. I am not going to call her a dairy maid as all the girls hated that soppy romantic title, and very few of them were maidens either. The bottles were washed by her calloused hand, made sore by hot water and caustic soda, using a funny cranked brush . In those days no self respecting man would willingly wash bottles. That was "wimmin's work". And it was quite a performance. First of all the bottles were rinsed out in cold water. Cold water had to be used otherwise the milk would stick to the sides Then the bottles were immersed, in their crates, in a big steel bath of hot water and caustic soda, taken out one at a time for brushing and put into another bath of cold water to rinse. The crates were then stacked into a steam chest and sterilised using the steam from the boiler. The steam chest room was the very best place to be in winter, it was like a holiday in summer in Torquay! The top of the metal steam chest was always cluttered up with everybody's wet overcoats and hats and smelly gum boots drying off. The farm cats used to love this place too as it was warm and always had a good supply of clothing to nest in. Many a litter of kittens started life on the top of the steam chest. The adult cats would fight over the used milk filter, the sile as we called it. It must have made good eating.

Depending on the nature, age and physical appearance of the lasses in the dairy, it was also the place where a great deal of chaffing, chatting up and sneaky goings-on happened too! A great place to have your tea and "snap", as mid-morning sandwiches were called. The girls all lived in the local villages and were well used to country humour and language. They soon became hardened and inured to ribald comments from the men, and could give as good as they got too. I have seen, on many occasions, a lad running out of the dairy, cap in hand, being chased by an irate, red faced and flustered lass, who, with her hands full of a crate of milk bottles, had been pinched or tweaked in places where young ladies shouldn't be tweaked but liked being tweaked! I've also seen lads run out of there holding other things besides their caps, having been whacked with a bottle brush.

The afternoon's milking was all bottled in the evening and, at about five o'clock the following morning, the milk roundsman would start his day. Our longest serving roundsman or milkman, or the one I can remember above all others was Tommy. Tommy was the spitting image of Tommy Steele, the pop singer. He was tall and fair, longish hair for those days, good looking in a pleasantly fresh-faced sort of way and a very happy-go lucky nature. He was always singing or whistling, knew everybody in the area by name, their problems, state of health and finances. He always beat the newspapers by days with the hatches, matches and despatches of the local population, not in a gossipy sort of way, you understand, but in an interested and informative manner. He was loved by the pensioners and older ladies and adored by the younger ones. He always had a pleasant word with everybody on the street and many a time was asked to deliver things from a mother to her daughter, and vice versa, somewhere else in the village. The other half of the team was Princess, a six year old chestnut mare with a white circle on the top of her head which looked like a tiara, hence the name. She was a sturdy legged animal, heavier than a hunter horse but lighter legged than the Shire horses used for the heavy work. Princess was housed for five nights of the week in the stable along with the other horses. She would always spend Saturday and Sunday nights out in the horse paddock when the weather was fine. When she was let out on a Saturday evening her first action was to charge around the paddock in a free and fanciful way, happy to be able to have a good gallop without the encumbrance of harness and the milk float. Sometimes, when she was feeling feisty on a Monday morning, she really took some catching which used to

irritate Tommy for the rest of the day, well until lunchtime anyway, by which time she had been forgiven.

Unless old Jim had done it, Tommy's first job in the morning was to harness up Princess and couple her into the milk float. A milk float was a fairly light and low cart with a wide entrance at the rear. It had two large, but narrow, cart wheels and Princess could move this lot along at quite a pace. Then he had to load up his milk crates and also some cans of milk as some customers would insist on sticking to their own milk containers. His change bag of money, the cream and eggs were all laid out ready for him to take from the house. Somebody always had to get up early to let Tommy in every morning of the year except Sundays and Christmas Day. By nine o'clock, Tommy had delivered his first load of milk, from last night's milking, and was back to collect the morning's milking. This, if all went according to plan, was bottled or in the churns and ready to go. Every day there had to be a surplus produced ready for Saturday as, without a delivery on Sunday, customers had to double up their orders for the weekend. That was not always a strict mathematical calculation either as "The family are coming round for tea on Sunday and so we need some extra". If they were going for tea somewhere, they still wanted their regular amounts. Customers also wanted fresh cream on a Saturday for the cake or scones that were going to be eaten. As you can imagine, all this required a great deal of forward production planning. Roll over enough bottled milk every day to be able to keep back a lot of the fresh milk for cream production on Friday evening.

Tommy and Princess were a wonderful team. Our milk round was rows of terraced houses mainly owned by the local colliery workers. The front doors of these houses opened straight onto the public pavement and the front steps were a source of pride and joy to the housewife. She could be found at least three times a week, cleaning and scrubbing that front step. They certainly didn't want their milk bottles making marks on the step and anyway, they didn't want their neighbours seeing how much milk they were taking or if they were having cream that weekend.

So, the milk had to be taken round the back. That meant transferring twelve bottles into a special hand held carrier, walking through the ginnel or passage between two rows of houses, depositing full bottles and collecting empties at each house. Now, by the time a row had been done, the horse and milk float should have been waiting at the starting point. Not Princess. She knew as soon as Tommy set off down the ginnel and would walk herself to the other end of the terrace and would be patiently waiting for Tommy to emerge. As soon as he climbed back into the float, she would set off without a word of command, for the next stopping point. This would allow Tommy to empty and recharge his carrier for his next walking trip. In all the time that Tommy and Princess worked together as a team, they never got involved in a traffic accident. The local "Bobby" wasn't too pleased about it but tolerated the situation because he was a customer too!

Saturday was a difficult day in Tommy's life. First of all he had a double delivery to make which really slowed him up. Secondly, as most of the miner customers were paid on a Friday evening, Saturday was the best and safest day to collect the money for the weeks' deliveries. By Monday, the money for the milk could, and more likely would, have found its way into the pub landlord's till. A special milk book was kept in which Tommy recorded who had bought what during the week and, despite the barest minimum of formal education, Tommy could calculate how much was owed faster than a computer. At the end of the day, it took several hours to balance the amount of money received back to the milk, cream and eggs taken from the dairy. Calculators were unheard of in those days and have you tried using a calculator, which relies on the decimal system, to add up in pounds, shillings and pence? Twelve pence to a shilling and twenty shillings to a pound? Tommy and the boss's wife could add up columns of £, s, d like lightning. Tommy was a good and faithful employee and it was a rare occasion if he was out more than a couple of bob either way. His job had its perks too. He was always offered more cups of tea and slices of cake than he had time or appetite for during his rounds. We always thought he was probably offered more than that by some of the attractive young wives who were his customers, but couldn't work out how he found the time.

During the school holidays he was always plagued by scores of young lads who wanted to help him. Really, all they wanted to do was hold the reins of the horse and pretend they were Roman charioteers as the horse always went home, with the now lighter float, at a good lick. I know that was the feeling because I did it too! It was maybe during the holidays with a lot of helpers that Tommy spent a little time on his "Public Relations"! I do know it happened because I can remember a big shindig once when an angry husband came to the farm one day looking for Tommy. I was too young then to be involved in such things so I can't remember what the outcome was. Tommy made an absolute fortune at Christmas time from the "Christmas Boxes" given to him from his loyal clientele. He deserved every penny he made.

If, for whatever reason, Princess couldn't do the milk run, then Tommy had a problem and always finished a lot later. We had a spare horse who could cope with the job but it took a second person to drive or lead the horse. If Tommy was ever sick or on holiday then the fun started. It didn't matter how long somebody had understudied him for before his annual holiday, the relief man, and the customers were always delighted to see him return to his familiar job. The girls couldn't do the job as the crates and milk carriers were quite heavy and catching and harnessing the horse was a handful.

Princess used to have a torrid time in winter with the icy roads, sometimes a couple of feet thick with snow, before the Council snow ploughs had made it out of bed. She had some special shoes fitted in winter with segs like climbing boots had on them, screwed into the shoe. This generally did stop her from slipping but I can remember being terrified of her falling especially leading her slowly down a couple of very steep hills on the milk round. If she did slip and fall, and she did on several occasions, it was a monster task to unhitch her with a very heavily loaded milk float wanting to slide down the hill of its own accord. It was on such occasions that Tommy appreciated his customers who would, without being asked, turn out in their curlers, dressing gowns and gum boots to help him. The worst scenes were when the float tipped up and the crates fell through the opening at the rear onto the road. There would be milk, glass and broken eggs everywhere to be swept up, which it quickly was by willing hands.

Princess was finally "pensioned" off at a ripe old age and such was the sentimentality attached to her that instead of the knackers yard, normal fate for retired work animals, she was kept on the farm where kids, like me, used to come in summer and ride her, bare backed and with only a head halter rope at a very gentle pace around the paddock. She was put into a small but special paddock in front of the house, where we had some apple trees, for a short while every day. She made short work of the windfalls and would, if they were not protected, steal the apples from the trees.

Princess was replaced by modern technology, a motorised, specially bodied milk float or van. The problem here was that Tommy couldn't drive and didn't have a licence. Although he really wanted to learn this new modern method, he had several run-ins with the driving examiner before he did eventually pass. He swore that the motorised unit was nowhere near as good as a horse because it wouldn't and couldn't think for itself, or move by itself to pick him up. He did admit that it was a bit better in winter when he could turn the heater on to warm himself up. And it didn't fall down on the slopes, especially when fitted with snow chains. But, whereas he had trouble some summer mornings catching Princess in the paddock, he also had trouble starting the engine in the early hours of a winter morning. That still made it thirty fifteen in the score! It was forty fifteen when the van had a puncture and game when it ran out of fuel. It was set and match to Princess when the van broke a half shaft going up a hill one day.

Life, death and procreation are very normal and natural happenings on a farm. Despite living every day with the animal side of it, human sexuality always plays a part when young, fit, red-blooded members of the opposite sex have to work together. Today, there would be hundreds of sexual harassment and sex discrimination cases, more than the courts of law could handle. The Land Girls, as they were called, were doing their bit for King and Country, and the lads were trying to do a bit for the Land Girls as well! Animals being born were a simple fact of life, literally. Everybody knew how and why pregnancies happened, there were no stories of birds and bees and gooseberry bushes and storks. Similarly, death was accepted too in a similar, and perhaps, simplistic and unemotional manner. When a calf was born with a deformity, five legs or two heads, it was just despatched with the minimum of fuss. We, as with all dairy farms, had plenty of cats. They were very necessary to keep the rats and mice from doing too much damage but could become very in-bred when the farm was a long way from the next habitation. When an in-bred litter was found or when the population became just too dense, all the litter except one would be drowned at birth. This, to a non country dweller, might seem a bit harsh but, which is better? A healthy population of cats or fifty diseased and malformed animals who would in all probability be stepped on by a cow before reaching the end of their natural life span?

When a cow comes into season she informs the entire world by trying to "ride" or by being ridden by the rest of the herd. This is very disruptive and the milk yields can drop off pretty drastically as the animals have other things than making milk on their minds that day. We had a bulling pen where the cow was introduced to the bull of our, not her, choice. We always had several bulls around. The Friesian bulls

were always called "Billy". We had two of these, Old Billy and Young Billy. Old Billy was an absolute monster, and when finally sent off for slaughter at the end of his career, weighed in at twenty six hundred weights, That's about two thousand nine hundred pounds! He was far too heavy to service all except the biggest cows. We used Young Billy for the smaller cows and on Old Billy's daughters. Later on we also had a Hereford bull and used these calves for beef production. We had one Young Billy who was rather a nasty piece of work, not uncommon in Friesians, who trapped one of the lads one day. He chased the lad into the corner of two buildings in the yard. The buildings were built out of Yorkshire granite and somehow the lad managed to climb up the stones out of harm's way. He was rescued by a contingent of people armed with pitchforks, brooms, shovels, muck forks and anything else that was close to hand. The bull was captured using a bull hook, a long pole with a hook in it that you have to slip into the bull's nose ring, and led back to his stall. We then asked the lad to show us how he had climbed up the wall and he couldn't do it! His adrenalin must have taken over, because he couldn't even remember getting up there.

The second time Young Billy misbehaved, he chased one of the lasses around the yard. She was rescued by the ever present sheepdog, Shep, who, by swinging on the bull's tail, a favourite trick of his, distracted the bull long enough for the lass to get away. That was the end of that Young Billy. It was generally agreed that he was going to lame somebody one day, plus, he was "black-legged" by the staff who refused to handle him. This meant the Boss had to do it himself and that wasn't really on. Young Billy became a vast amount of dog food.

Milk is one of Nature's finest foods. Most people consume it in one form or another all their lives. Fresh milk, powdered milk, condensed milk, skimmed milk, cream, butter, cheese, yoghurt, high fat, low fat, no fat, homogenised, pasteurised, hot, cold, ice cream and so on. All this from a humble, lowly old cow. I can remember making cream on the farm, and what a performance that was too. First, we had to take warm milk straight from the cows. We had a machine which consisted of, seemingly, hundreds of conical shaped, stainless steel plates, all fixed closely together on a shaft. The milk was poured in at the top and came out as cream on one side and skimmed milk on the other. The pain was, that this was a hand cranked machine which took mighty muscles to turn it at the right speed. It had to be turned fast enough for a bell to ring every turn of the handle. Even the strongest and fittest of the men could stand about five minutes of this cranking before he was worn out. Another man would take over, on the move, without letting the speed drop or else all the skimmed milk went back into the machine again. I think it must have worked on centrifugal speed somehow with the cream being the heaviest, being flung to the ends of the cones. Afterwards it was about a two hour job to dismantle the machine and individually wash each of the many cones, sterilise them and reassemble the machine. But was it ever good cream at the end of the day! Especially on a lemon sponge cake which I used to, and still do, absolutely drool over.

I am sure that both my readers have enjoyed the James Herriot books about the life of a veterinary surgeon based in Yorkshire. We had to be the farmers he based a lot of his books around. We were really dreadful. There seemed to be certain rules regarding calling the vet.

These were the "Ten Commandments when dealing with Veterinaries".

One; always wait until the animal is a death's door, then call the vet. Then you could blame him for killing your animal and have an argument over the bill when it arrived.

Two; as medicines were expensive, always cut the recommended dosage down by half. By doing this you had enough for the next sick animal without calling the vet out. If the animal didn't improve, then you could blame the vet for not giving you the right dosage in the first instance.

Three; always wait to call the vet out on a Saturday afternoon or Sunday morning. That way he was usually delayed in getting to you so you could say that the animal was saveable when you had called him but because he was late, that's why the beast died.

Four; always save up a few cases for the vet so that you got several consultations for the price of one visit.

Five; always, on principle, ask the vet for any free samples of anything. You don't know when it will come in handy later even if the medicine had expired or if you had forgotten what it was for.

Six; always take him to the animal you originally called him out for by the longest route, around all the other animals. That way he might be able to see another sick beast without you calling him out again.

Seven; never supply him with warm water and a clean towel. He can manage with a bucket of cold water from the outside trough just like you do and wipe his hands on a piece of old sack or down his overalls. Otherwise you will make him soft.

Eight; when the animal is in the field, always go in his car. After all you have paid for the mileage haven't you?

Nine; always invite him back for a cup of tea when he has finished. That way you can pump him for information regarding the latest methods and farming techniques, who is doing what in the area and who has got what diseases and problems.

Ten; never pay the bill promptly. That way he will be forced to come back to collect his money and while he is there show him the results of his handiwork or pump him for information again. Also, always ask for a discount on the bill.

There were many home remedies for cattle to be tried before you called the vet. We had many strange concoctions which the maker always laid claim that it solve any problem. The favourite was a couple of spoons of sulphanilamide powder mixed with old bitter beer from the pub, add to it some ginger powder, ("that'll warm 'er up"), a couple of spoons of castor oil or some kaolin and morphine powder depending on her current bowel condition, and a handful of aspirin tablets, crushed, if you felt whatever she had, looked sore. Mix the concoction into a pan and warm it up on the stove. Then, using an old milk bottle, hold the cow's head under your arm, shove the bottle into the corner of its mouth on top of its tongue and fight like Hell until it had all gone down. This should be repeated until the cow is at death's door, then refer to the Commandments above!

Sometimes it was just common-or-garden bloat that the animal had. Cows have a problem that, on certain rations of fresh green clover, they get a very uncomfortable amount of gas trapped in the stomach. Which one of the four stomachs it was didn't really matter. The poor animal would blow up like a balloon and you always thought that if there was a stiff wind she would probably float away. The remedy for this was an instrument called a trocar. The trocar consisted of two pieces of stainless steel pipe. The outer pipe narrowed at the bottom with a fine cutting edge honed on the base. At the top of this pipe was a flat flange about three or four inches in diameter. The second pipe was a tight push fit into the first pipe. The bottom end blocked off and had a flat topped handle on the outside or top of it. The instrument was held, sharp side to the animal, against the bloated side of the cow and given a very sharp and smart crack with the palm of the hand or a piece of flat wood. The trocar would penetrate the hide and gut of the cow and the flange would stop you from losing it inside the animal. Then the centre piece was withdrawn. Now, if you were standing in direct line of fire, the chances were that nobody would go within twenty paces of you for the next week as, usually, a torrent of gas, digestive juices, fodder and anything else inside the cow would shoot out like an oil geyser. The stench was enough to turn the stomach of the strongest person. Quite often, vegetative material would block the bottom of the pipe and the centre would have to be inserted again and given a little jiggle. The same geyser effect would be evidenced. When satisfied that this new found gas field had settled to a quiet hiss, the centre could be left out for a day or so until the animal had sorted its own digestive system out. Then the outer bit could be removed.

On occasions it was a bit easier to attack the problem from the other end, the mouth. We used to feed cattle on waste or sub standard potatoes and sometimes they would get a whole potato stuck in their throat. Without the ability to release the stomach gas with a regular good healthy belch, the animal would blow up. I once had this happen and shoved a length of hose pipe down its mouth. This had a startling result as the potato, under some considerable pressure, became dislodged and shot out like a Scud Missile at me. The next time this happened I made sure that I was out of the line of fire first.

Cows' feet were another problem for two reasons. Having to stand in one place for most of the time during winter, the cows rear hooves would grow to look like a pair of Ali Baba pointed shoes. The remedy was very easy, take a saw and saw them off. Toe nail cutting time! This sounds easy but remember you are dealing with the kicking end mechanism of the cow. Answer, tie a rope to the beam above the animal and attach the other end to its foot. Haul on the rope until the leg is in the air. Then with one person holding the twitching, I-am-trying-to-kick-you leg, trim off the offending toe growth with a pruning saw. If you kept all the bits and rendered them down you could end up with some super wood glue, that is, if you could stand the smell of them cooking.

The second most common problem was foot rot between the hooves. This usually occurred during wet summers when the cows were paddling in wet grass and mud for month after month. The animal

would start limping and you could usually smell the rot too. We used to slide a rope into the cleft between the hooves and saw it backwards and forwards to clean it out and get rid of the decaying flesh. Then put the foot into a bucket of warm water and strong disinfectant and hang onto it for as long as possible. It worked in ninety five percent of cases.

With all these local animal fixing home remedies, you can see why vets were treated with considerable disdain if they couldn't effect a miracle cure overnight. With hindsight, I take my hat off to those fine professional gentlemen who served us. They really had a hard time of it especially from us! Things have changed now, modern drugs make short work of the common problems we had. The trouble is that every time they come up with a new drug for an old problem, some silly scientist goes and finds a few more diseases or ailments. When will it ever stop I wonder.

A shaggy dog story told to me years ago. Two old horse handlers were sitting in the snug of the village pub, one cold evening, puffing at their pipes and quaffing their ale. Conversation was always a bit slow and laconic. The younger of the two put down his pint pot and said, "My 'orse, she be lame".

The older one cleaned out his pipe, refilled it and eventually got it going to his satisfaction.

"Oh, aar?" queried the older fellow.

"Aar, she be lame", repeated the younger.

Nearly an hour of silent drinking and pipe puffing went by.

Then the older man said, " My 'orse, she were lame too".

Another pint of ale was purchased.

"Oh, aar?" said the younger, with interest in his voice.

"Aar, she were" was the confirming response after a while.

Another good half hour passed in comfortable silence.

"Ah gave 'ee turp'n'tine", said the older fellow.

"Oh, aar", said the younger, "turp'n'tine", he repeated and vegetated on that for a long while.

The following week, the two of them were back in the snug, enjoying their beer in front of the fire.

The younger of the two opened the conversation.

“My ‘orse, her wot were lame”, he started. Twenty minutes passed.

“She died”, he finally came out with.

“Aar”, said the offerer of advice.

Another twenty minutes passed.

“So did mine”.

In spite of that shaggy dog tale, many of the old remedies did actually, remarkably, work!

Today’s milk production methods are much more refined than those of yesterday and anybody farming in the old fashioned ways would soon be out of business today. Even the Amish, or Anabaptist people of Pennsylvania who stick to their old ways, are having a tough time of it with fewer and fewer of them able to maintain their livelihoods from farming. By the same token though, there is a move to produce foodstuffs without the aid of modern fertilizers and chemicals. The organic farmer. I bet he doesn’t milk his cows by hand though!

Next time you have a cup of tea or a bowl of your favourite breakfast cereal, spare a thought for the old cow . On your next visit through the countryside, spend a couple of minutes watching a herd of cattle.

You, as I do, will find them fascinating animals. Should you happen to pop into a country pub for supper, have a look around for the old cow man. He’ll be there somewhere. But especially, watch out for two old chaps who smell of horses a bit!!

Chapter 4

Root Crops

Collecting turnips, swedes or mangold wurzels from the fields in autumn and early winter was a terrible job which, try as I would to be somewhere else at the time, I always seemed to get "volunteered" for service. Because of the wet conditions in the fields it was far better to take a horse and cart to lead the turnips. At this stage in my life I was too young to pull the turnips, a horrible job lined up for me for the future. Mangolds are sensitive to frost and had to be stored before the onset of winter in things called "mangold pies" A "pie" was a structure built out of straw sheaves or bales and the roots were thrown into an elongated pyramid shape and covered up against the frost and the rain. If it was not covered up correctly the mangolds would get frosted and rot with a terrible stench. The rotted roots still had to be removed and thrown back onto the fields as manure. When stored correctly, mangolds would outlast turnips or swedes and give the cattle something to eat just before spring and the new growth of grass arrived.

The actual work of pulling or lifting roots was a back breaker. The roots grow half in and half out of the ground and a reasonable turnip can weigh over ten pounds. The tops were usually wet and it was always cold. Despite wearing gloves, you're hands were usually cold and wet in a very short space of time. The trick was to pull the root out of the ground with the left hand, trim the soil and straggling roots off with one blow of the turnip knife, a vicious looking object with a hook at one end, and then toss the root into a row, slicing the top off as it was in motion. The root ideally came to rest in a windrow, putting eight rows of turnips into one windrow, and the tops were dropped below your feet. As there was only a margin of about two inches from the shoulder of the root to your fingers it was a dead certainty that at some stage, you would miss the root and hit your hand. If it didn't cut you through the glove, it was still extremely painful, especially with your hand being almost numb from cold.

The windrows had to be laid out precisely so that the horse could walk without stomping the roots back into the ground. Mostly, the horses were well trained and used to this sort of job and could be made to move and stop by voice commands, "Gee" for right, "Harve" for left, "Whoa" to stop and a tongue clicking sound something like "tchee, tchee" to start them walking. By calling "Back, Back" a good horse would also go into reverse but the direction was not always as certain as going forwards. Good as they were, the horses attention could stray too, probably thinking about their oats or something, and would have to be brought into line again. As the weather was invariably wet, we sometimes had a great deal of bother getting the cart out of the field. This involved a lot of pushing and urging the horse to make a greater effort. To help, we would pull on the wheel struts or push from behind. I know where the slapstick comedians got that act of falling down into the mud. It was normally as a result of your boots being so deep in the mud that you couldn't get them out fast enough when the cart eventually started to move. A good cursing session or total merriment always followed one of these acts, depending who had fallen.

Looking back at such root crops I now wonder if they were really worth it. A turnip is about ninety five percent water. The field had to be very carefully prepared to a fine tilth to take the seed, the size of a pin head, planted just under the surface of the soil, in straight lines and at the right time of the year. Before precision planters were freely available, the rows of emerging roots had to be thinned and spaced out. This was done by man power using swan necked hoes. The inter-row weeds could usually be taken out by mechanical means using a tractor or horse powered cultivator. That was a very specialised job calling for a lot of experience and accuracy as any slight deviation weeded the crop out too! The hand hoeing usually had to be repeated depending on the weather. The wetter the season, the more vigorously the weeds would grow. You had to wait for a dry day as the wet soil would cling to the hoe head, making it like a battering ram, and heavy too. Also, weeding in wet weather is a good way of transplanting, not killing, weeds. Because of this, and before chemicals were used to control weeds, there was a good chance that if the weather was too wet, the weeds won. Being a root crop the plant needed an adequate and frequent supply of water to grow or face a crop failure. However impossible this water balance may seem to be, especially considering the vagaries of the English and Yorkshire weather, it was remarkable that the tonnage of crop eventually removed was so back breaking. After lifting and carting home, the roots still had to be put through a turnip chopper to slice them

into slivers small enough for cattle to eat without getting bits stuck in their gullets. All that work to feed animals ninety five percent water. Why didn't we just show them the water trough and a bit of straw?

I must admit, a slice of freshly cut sweet turnip, raw of course, always did taste rather good, even to me. But please, don't ever try to give it to me cooked. It's disgusting!

Chapter 5

Sheep And Sheepdogs

Although we lived on the relative lowlands of Yorkshire, sheep became part of our lives as much as they were to our neighbours a little higher up on the moors and in the Dales. The Yorkshire Moors are renowned for their sheep; after all, other than grouse and partridge, they are about the only creatures who can live up there.

We didn't start keeping sheep until I was nearly an adolescent, so much of what follows is a little higher up in my mental filing cabinet. We had two breeds of sheep, and they were so completely different in character and nature, that it was like having another specie of animal. First we had the Border Leicester ewes, our own small breeding flock. The Border Leicester is a big and rather arrogant looking animal, with a long curved Roman nose and a white face. They had to lift their heads up and peer down their noses to look at you and that added to their disdainful look. They were fairly docile animals, content to sleep and eat most of the day without causing too much of a problem. They produced thick, tight, curly wool in sufficient quantities to keep themselves warm during our winters. We normally used a Suffolk ram on them as this seemed to produce the hybrid vigour needed to produce good strong well boned and meaty lambs. These sheep were with us all the year round and produced their lambs on the coldest wettest days, or usually nights, of late December or early January.

The other flock was a temporary one, but the one that gave us the most headaches. In July, August or September, depending on the season and weather conditions, the hill farmers from the moors would send their crops of young lambs to the markets. These farmers knew that they would not be able to take their lambs as far as slaughter weight as they would have run out of food for them, and normally, their kind of country precluded them from growing fodder crops. Up in the hills they would have a battle to produce hay, as, for the majority of the Spring and early Summer, it would rain three days out of five. Hay made under those conditions totally lacks nutrition and is very unpalatable to animals.

Now because of these severe weather conditions, the hill farmer bred a completely different type of animal. Not for him the "soft" lowland breeds but an animal that could stand sub zero temperatures and wet weather for long spells at a time. Depending on his preference he could have a variety of breeds or cross bred ewes, specially adapted to these conditions.

Sheep breeds fall into three major types, Longwools, Short wools and Mountain Breeds and a fourth, a Crossbred animal, being a combination of any of the main three.

Longwools are such breeds as our Border Leicesters, Lincolns, Cotswolds, Kent and Romney Marsh. Being lowland sheep, they are, generally speaking, big animals. They produce long, and very good quality wool, much in demand for the finest worsted material. Their meat is usually a bit on the tough and grainy side and tends to be a bit flavourless too. Also, they go to fat very quickly unless left on barren ground, in which case, they were not the butcher's first choice.

The Shortwools are, as the name implies, a closer wooled animal, neat, compact, docile and relatively easy to manage. These have among their number such breeds as the Suffolks,

Norfolks, Hampshire Downs and Dorset. They produce a very good quality of meat as well as a good fleece. They are more of a lowland than upland sheep and are well suited to being kept in pastures and behind fences.

The Mountain Breeds are a different matter altogether. Physically, they are a lot smaller than the other main categories and have the inborn ability to survive the poor grazing and harsh weather conditions of their mountains. You will have heard of such breeds as Swaledale, Lonks, Cheviots, Dartmoor and Shetland. Their wool is very coarse but ideal for carpets and Harris Tweed. Their meat is sweet, full of flavour and not too fatty either. Most of them have horns too, unlike the softer lowland varieties.

The fourth general classification is the Cross Breed and, as the name implies, there are a multitude of cross breeds. Pure bred flocks of sheep are akin to raising pedigree animals. A pleasure to have and somebody has got to maintain the purity of the breed but, generally speaking, a cross bred will outperform a pure bred animal in almost every way and can be selected to suit your personal conditions and style of management. Without the pure bred animals there wouldn't be the parent flocks to produce the cross breeds from. Such names a Half Breed, Mashams, Mules and Grey Faced will, I am sure, be familiar to many people.

Before we go any further, let's get a bit of sheep terminology sorted out. The term "lamb" can mean different things to different people, depending on which part of the country you are in. In some places, a baby sheep is a lamb until it is weaned while we called them lambs until they came on heat for the first time at about nine to eleven months old. After this they became, at some non-prearranged time, hoggs. By non-prearranged, I mean that one day we were calling them lambs and the next we called them hoggs. When do you stop calling a boy, a boy, a young man and then a man? If the sheep were of the male sex they were called ram lambs or ram hoggs. Those that had been castrated were called wethers. Females were ewe lambs when young, ewe hoggs when a bit older and then ewes when they had their first lambs. When they had been sheared the males were called shearling rams or wethers and the females, gimmers. Some other names are used depending on the part of the country the sheep came from and, if in doubt it was always better to show a little ignorance and have the terminology cleared up otherwise you could be buying something else!

Like cattle, sheep develop their permanent teeth at a fixed time in their lives. Being ruminants, sheep do not have any top teeth but a bony pad. At twelve to fifteen months old the first pair of full teeth would replace the centre milk teeth and were followed, at about six monthly intervals, by another pair, one each side of the first pair. So at two years and nine months of age, a sheep would have a "full mouth" as it was called. After that, she was aged according to the number of times she had been sheared, a two shear, four shear, five shear, and so on.

Sheep are usually clipped for their wool for the first time in the summer, at the age of about fifteen months old. Being lambs in their first summer there is little or nothing to clip that first year. Shearing sheep is jolly hard work, made to look easy by the Australian shearers. They get so much practice with their vast flocks that it is not surprising that they are always world champion shearers. Our flock was not very big so we didn't get enough practice to be anything more than only just proficient. You have to pick a nice warm day to shear sheep. That way you sweat more and get smellier as the day goes on! Also the sheep have to be dry or the wool is down graded. We used to clip sheep with hand clippers, the things people use these days as lawn trimmers that look like funny scissors. That was very slow and wrist breaking work. If you could manage to do ten to fifteen sheep a day, you were doing well. To put that into perspective, the Aussie shearers with mechanical clippers do several hundred in an eight hour day! The clippers were also dangerous too as they had sharp points on them, necessary to get into the fleece. If you didn't fetch blood from almost every sheep you sheared it was a miracle. Bad cuts would be liberally daubed with Stockholm tar afterwards. The sheep I did went away looking like a tar-macadam road after I had finished hacking at them. It was a marvellous day when we bought a small electric powered set of clippers. Then I could make them bleed faster!

To start with, you have to catch the sheep and drag her to a cleaned off area, kicking and protesting as only sheep can do. Or it was passive resistance, locking her legs tight and having to be hauled to the shearing spot. The sheep then had to be up-ended, sat on its bottom and placed between your legs, belly forward. The clipping starts with taking off the belly fleece and then going down one side until you get to its rear end. The sheep then gets rolled around in a slow barrel roll as you clip, trying to leave the fleece on one side at all times, and away from the animal. Sounds easy, and it is until you get to the part in the roll where the sheep thinks that it wants to stand up. Brute force usually overcomes such actions. Eventually, the sheep is shorn and you can try to straighten your back out to somewhere near normal vertical position, if you can put up with the pain of doing so. How people shear sheep for a livelihood beats me. They must have incredibly strong backs to be able to withstand that constant stooping and bending.

The fleece is then wrapped and rolled up in a special way to keep it all together in one piece. The rolled fleece is tied up with the last scraggy tailing pieces which are twisted to form a rope. The fleeces are then baled up and off to the wool merchant. All good clean fun you think? The grease has "risen" in the fleece before you clip it and having the animal between your legs has given your trousers a good coating of sheep fleece grease. It's too hot to wear an overall and if you wear shorts to work in, like many of the Aussies do, the thorns lodged in the fleece tear your legs to bits.

The wool industry of Yorkshire is a long established business. It started and proliferated there because of the adequate quantities of clean and soft water from the moorlands, essential to a wool processor as wool needs a lot of washing to remove the natural greases before spinning. The softer the water, the less washing chemicals were required and therefore the lower the costs of production. Also the streams used to be the source of motive power for the machinery used in the mills.

Despite the advances made today in the production of synthetic fibres, pure wool takes an awful lot of beating for warmth, durability, and water repellant properties. It has the ability to "breathe" when next to the skin unlike many of the man-made fibres of today which draw the perspiration out of you in an uncomfortable manner. Some sheep are kept primarily for their wool, notable among these are the Merinos of Australia. Some don't have any wool to speak of at all, like the Persian sheep of the Middle East and parts of Africa. Most English sheep are kept for both their wool and their meat. Wool terminology is also a complicated matter but, as a farmer you had to know some of this terminology to be able to work out what kind of sheep to keep. Wool has certain standard classifications. The length of the fibre, which can range from one inch to an amazing twenty four inches, is obviously of great importance. The strength of the wool can vary enormously too and naturally, for the wool spinner and weaver, the stronger the wool, the less breaks he gets when manufacturing the fibre. The strength is also related to the fineness of the wool and the finer it is the softer the finished article. Then there is the "crimp" or elasticity of the wool which allows a woollen garment to maintain its shape after manufacture. The production of good or poor wool is very much in the hands of the farmer, after having discounted breed variations. If sheep became sick or undernourished, this would show up much later as a weakening of each fibre at exactly the time that such malnutrition occurred. After shearing, the fleece could literally fall in half, having broken at these weak points. Quite often sheep who got into this condition would shed the outer layer of wool in the field and be left with a shorter, and therefore, less productive fleece at shearing time. It was worth walking over the fields with a sack to collect these bits as they were still worth something in the market place. The colour of the wool is also important as it is impossible to get a naturally black sheep's wool to make a white sweater!

Back to our Mountain sheep. Their biggest problem was that they had never seen a hedge or a fence in their lives. They used to roam the moors at will. They thought stone walls were there to shelter them from storms, not to restrict their movement. These sheep didn't even understand English, or our kind of Yorkshire English anyway. I will confess that I had trouble sometimes understanding what the shepherd from the far flung moorland areas was saying, his dialect being so different to ours. They understood dogs though. More about them anon.

The big advantage to these sheep was that, having been brought up on the moors, they had a frame of fairly solid, if small, bone, and, when given access to some decent food, put on meat at a very fast rate. They were also relatively cheap as the buyer knew that the seller had to sell and couldn't take them home again.

These things were wild. Unlike the lowland sheep who always had food in the same field and therefore stuck together or "flocked" well, the Mountain sheep roam the moors in ones and twos, spread over many square miles. When afraid, they will flock together, probably a natural reaction, strength in numbers, and the only thing which can put them into this state is a good sheepdog. I suppose that way back when in time, the natural predator of sheep would have been the wolf. A sheep dog, especially the Border Collies used today are a far cry from a wolf but who knows how the sheep sees the dog? Working with these wild things was an exhausting affair for our dogs. They were used to the more docile lowland breeding flock which would collectively tug their forelocks and do exactly as they were told. Not so the mountain sheep. After a strenuous run around the field, the dogs would have the sheep nicely bunched together when some renegade animal would make a break for it. Once you lost one, you usually lost the lot and those things can run like hares. As a mob, they would congregate themselves at the far end of the field, the furthest corner away from the gate that you were trying to get them through and so, it was, start again.

We used to buy several hundred of these little beggars from one or more market sales, specially set up for store lambs as they were called. Sometimes we would go as far north as Scotland to buy them, but transport had to be considered in the costing. These poor, half starved little things would look so pitiful in the market pens, so sweet and docile. They were loaded onto big trucks, specially designed with several decks for carrying sheep. Depending where they were purchased, it made good sense, as far as the transport costs were concerned, to make sure that we bought enough to fill the truck and no more. They were counted onto the truck at loading and counted again when they were off loaded at the farm. Some truck drivers were also partial to a bit of fresh lamb too!

Counting sheep is not quite as easy as we are led to believe. I am sure that we all have pictures in our minds of little woolly things, gently jumping over a log, slowly and one at a time. That's the sort of image we are asked to conjure up when we can't go to sleep. Who ever made that suggestion had never counted sheep in his life. Despite placing a restriction at the exit from the truck, they would all try to charge out of this little opening at the same time and would go bounding out in threes and fours. Sometimes they would be either so happy to get out of the truck, or so afraid at what was going on, that they would take flying leaps into air, over the heads of their travelling mates. Now imagine yourself trying to count this hoard of charging woolly backs and you will soon realise that you were incredibly lucky if you were satisfied with the result on the first go. If not, then the procedure would be to flock them together in a corner of the field and let them "escape" from the flock one at a time. As we counted our sheep virtually every day, they soon got wise to this move and would eventually reach a stage of partial training, about as good as we were ever going to get. We had to count the blessed things every day because it was not unusual for a couple of them to be trapped in the hawthorn hedgerow by their long wool. A sheep trapped like this would soon die of exhaustion. Why they always spent a lot of time foraging in the hedgerows seemed ridiculous when the field they were in consisted of several varieties of pasture grass and clover, the likes of which they had never seen on the moors. I suppose it was for a change of diet and some special succulent plant which had taken their fancy. As they got fatter, the width of their backs meant that if they ever rolled onto their backs, especially in a small hollow in the field, they couldn't get back on their feet again. A sheep doing this, being a ruminant, would blow up like a balloon in a few hours and could be dead within twelve hours.

Bringing these animals on to new and verdant pastures was a tricky thing. Their stomachs were not used to the lushness of pasture offered to them and if care wasn't taken they could wind up with scours or bloat. They were introduced first of all to a field which had been heavily grazed by the cattle or, if corn harvest was early enough, on to the straw stubble left after harvest. Then their stomach flora would get used to the new diet and away they went. First thing we had to do with them was dose them for some of the vast number of parasites and diseases which sheep get. We had special sheep handling pens and facilities on the farm for this but we had to get the sheep to the farm buildings. The sheep hadn't a clue where they were going and would lead us a merry dance as they were driven down the road, getting into gardens and going down any side road that wasn't guarded.

I remember one charging into the little Post Office one day and causing a great deal of consternation among the old ladies lined up to collect their pensions. What made it worse was that the weather hadn't been too good and the sheep were wet through. The poor animal got such a fright when it bounded through the door that it slipped and fell, rolling on its side like a barrel, knocking into one old lady who promptly followed it to the floor. There were skirts and petticoats and wet sheep and sheep muck all over the place after this little episode. From the screams and peals of laughter, shouting and banging that was coming from the Post Office you would have thought two masked men were in there robbing the place and having their evil way with the ladies. Being country folk and being Yorkshire, they accepted this with a phlegmatic approach. "It's alright Luv, am not 'urt and it's only me owld coat anyway. It dun't matter, gerroff and fetch it back". The startled animal had shot out of the Post Office like a rocket and was going at a very fast four footed gallop down the road, in the opposite direction to the rest of the flock who were by now a hundred yards away.

It took me about two hours to eventually catch the little tearaway, having chased it on foot into the next village, about a mile and a half away. Eventually it made its way into somebody's garden where, aided by a couple of young lads we managed to trap it. The next problem was what to do with it now. Unlike dogs, sheep don't take very kindly to being walked on a leash and I certainly wasn't going to be seen trying to do that. I had my reputation to think about! Eventually I walked home and we took the car down, threw the lamb in the boot and slammed the lid on it. When we drove it into the field, having the perspicacity to close the gate behind us, as we opened the boot lid the lamb shot into the air like a cork from a champagne bottle. It ran bleating for twenty yards, stopped and looked back at us with, what seemed to me like a cheeky grin on its face as if to say "That was a bit of fun wasn't it?" and sauntered off to join its mates.

Once we had the sheep in the yard we let them settle down and went for lunch. An hour later we went back to the yard to find lambs everywhere. We had some stone steps which led into the corn chambers. There was one flight of steps going up to the first floor which was totally unprotected by railings or bars. These steps were full of lambs. There was a low wall, about three feet high, dividing the yard from the back garden of a cow man's cottage . That was also covered with lambs and some of the lambs had got into his garden. When we arrived, unexpectedly, back at the yard, with a very excited dog zig-zagging behind our heels, these lambs got a mighty fright. The ones on the wall all took off into the garden; the ones on the steps simply launched themselves into the air, hitting the ground on all fours, just like cats. I was certain that we were going to have several broken legs to contend with, but, with their moorland training not yet forgotten, these little things took it all as a matter of course. We then had fun catching the ones in the garden and throwing them back into the yard. It must have been all of five years later when we had a new cow man who really took pride in his garden and grew a lot of vegetables there, that the garden wall got itself raised one summer.

This little fiasco was repeated several times a year and for years on end, each time, and each year the little blighters would come up with a few new tricks. One trick, which cost us, was that the door at the top of the chamber steps was fastened with a simple hook, fairly low down on the door. Somehow, and everybody swears that the door hook was fastened, they managed to get the door open. Several of them got into the corn chamber and proceeded to gorge themselves on fresh wheat. They were like kids let loose in a cake shop. Three of them blew up from the corn and we lost two of the three lambs. The hook was moved higher and a second bolt was also fitted to the door. That caused problems of its own as everybody was now so conscious of ensuring the door was bolted, that on several occasions we managed to lock somebody into the chamber, and that was the only door in and out! I am not sure people were not locked in on purpose too sometimes!

Having been raised on the moors these lambs had hard little hooves. Despite the wet weather that usually prevails up there, the ground is either stony or well drained enough for surface water to quickly soak in. Moving them down to lower and less well drained soils always caused them to get sore and infected feet. To fix them, we walked the lambs through a foot bath with a strong disinfectant in it several times a season. Any really lame ones had to be caught and given individual attention. This involved catching the lamb and sitting it on its bottom, and then, holding it tightly between your legs, you were able to pare and medicate the foot. When the sheep were dry, this wasn't too bad but if they had to be handled when wet, it was another matter altogether. We had several pairs of waterproof trousers which helped to keep the water off but, being made out of a plastic coated material, it was very difficult to keep enough purchase on the animal using only the knees. After such sessions we were always stiff the next day in most peculiar places, like the inside of the thighs. The married men used to complain that it ruined their sex lives for a few days. The unmarried men daren't say a word for fear of causing rumours, gossip and endless questioning from the other men!

The most important tool for these days was the pocket knife. No self respecting cow man or shepherd was ever without his knife. It was always put into the same pocket of his choice, usually the right hand trouser pocket, and went everywhere with him, even to church on a Sunday. The knife had to be easily accessible as, with a lamb or full grown ewe between your legs, probably struggling too, you wanted to be able to get at it quickly to trim off any offending bits of hooves and to scrape out the rotten bits of flesh between the hooves too. This was the same knife that after a cursory wipe on the sleeve or trouser leg, would be used to divide out an apple amongst your mates. Never heard of anybody catching foot rot from doing that. We always blamed our foot rot from wearing Wellington boots with permanently damp socks in them. It must have been something to do with the shape of my feet but I could never prevent my socks from winding up in an uncomfortable bunch around my toes. Wellies are sock killers anyway, rubbing the heels out in next to no time. They are also leg hair killers, they rub the hair to death around the top of the calf muscle. This was alright in winter but you looked very silly when in a bathing costume or shorts in summer!

A new knife was always inspected and handled by everybody, all the lads making appreciative noises. If anybody ever gave you a knife though, you had to give him a penny in return. Superstition said that if you didn't you would fall out with the giver and cut yourself with the knife. Your knife was always kept sharp. There is probably nothing as frustrating as trying to cut something with a blunt knife. It's also dangerous as a blunt knife will probably slip off whatever it is you are trying to cut but somehow, it manages to take your skin off. They were badly abused too, being used as a screw driver, wire cutters, hammers for tapping in little nails that stuck out and threatened to rip your trousers, shorting out the starter solenoid, and cutting a plug of tobacco for the pipe. In fact, what would we do without one? They got lost or mislaid on rare occasions which caused a general hunt to take place, but more often, they just got worn out from constant use and sharpening. Old habits die hard, and I still carry a pocket knife everywhere, much to the amusement of my family who, never the less, always seem to be the ones who want to use it.

In the winter, when the grass had stopped growing, we fed the lambs on a diet of turnips or swedes and sometimes, kale. This was supplemented with some hay and to finish them off for the butcher, a barley based, home mixed cereal ration. The root crops were a pain. There are two ways of feeding sheep on roots, take the roots to the sheep or take the sheep to the roots. The former method is labour intensive, very arduous, backbreaking work. It involved having to pull the roots out by hand and load them onto a tractor or horse and cart. As ground conditions were often muddy and wet, the chances of getting bogged down in the field were always pretty good. Also the amount of soil compaction was high and this used to show up in the retarded growth of the next crop. Last but not least, where did you want the sheep manure at the end of the day? So, we used to take the sheep to the roots.

This was, initially, expensive in capital terms as the first thing to be done was to fence the entire field perimeter with sheep netting. Using bill hooks and slashers, the sides of the hedge would be trimmed and straightened. Sheep netting is made out of galvanised wire, about four feet high and bought in rolls of fifty yards. Wooden stakes or posts were knocked in, as close to the hedge as possible and in a fairly straight line. The easiest way to do this was to load all the stakes on a trailer or cart and put one strong man to stand on the cart.

We had big, heavy, wooden headed hammers, bound with metal hoops. The hoops stopped the hammer head from splitting and, unlike a metal hammer, using a wooden hammer stopped the top of the stake from splitting. One man would line up and position the stake in the ground. The man on the cart would wield the hammer, giving the stake some mighty blows, until it was driven securely in the ground and to the right depth. The first man had to hold onto the stake to prevent it from going in cockeyed and this was something of a dangerous task, depending on the proficiency of the man with the hammer. If the man on the ground didn't have faith in the man with the hammer he was in danger of getting a broken arm at worst, and a lot of new skin growth at best! The old saying, "When I nod my head you hit it" was close to the mark as the positioning man had to indicate when he was satisfied with the location of the point before the first blow was struck. It did happen that a slightly off centre blow would split the stake top, causing the hammer head to slip and go lower than ever intended.

When this happens there is no warning and no time to warn. If your concentration lapsed for a second it could be quite painful. On such occasions, there was a good chance of the hammer man falling off the trailer as the follow-through of the heavy hammer pulled him off. You couldn't let go of the hammer for fear of it hitting your work mate so you followed it, trying hard on the way down to avoid being impaled on the end of the stake. A more usual result of such a fall was colliding with some force with the other man and both of you sitting in a tangle in the mud. Language used after such happenings could make your hair curl. The perpetrator would get cursed, the stake, hammer, horse, (if it had moved slightly), weather, hedge, and every sheep ever put on this earth all came in for it with a vengeance. As a growing lad, I really came in for an education not available in any college on earth!

The netting would then be stapled to the fencing stakes and woe betide you if you knocked the staple too far into the wood as somebody had to take them all out again once that field had been eaten off by the sheep. As these jobs always took place in winter, it was invariably done with a pair of very cold hands, so cold that you couldn't feel if you had the staple between your fingers or not. You always felt the hammer when you miss-hit the staple though. This would cause some hilarity from your mate, as a good sharp crack from a hammer usually resulted in the hammer being dropped in the mud as one hand clutched the other to ease the pain . "I never felt a thing" your mate would laughingly say. For speed and efficiency, spare staples were held in between the teeth. Try saying "ouch" without opening your mouth. It's like trying to sneeze without closing your eyes. So, bend down, scratch in the mud to find all the dropped staples, and restart the job again.

Eventually you would, by perseverance, get around the field and back to the starting point. Next move was to decide how many rows of swedes to allocate to the lambs for this "bite". If there were too few given, the job had to be repeated in the very near future. If too many, the lambs would foul and stand on a lot of them which was a waste. Having estimated the amount, the strip fence was then erected. This was done in a fairly similar manner to putting up the boundary fence, by knocking in stakes for the netting to hang from. The difference was in the method of hanging the wire. As the wire had to be taken down in about four days' time, it was put up using baling twine to hold it. Pieces of baling twine, meticulously kept from every bale of hay and straw, cut only at the knots, were kept in sacks hanging up all around the farm for this purpose. They were cut up into short pieces, tied into bundles and could be attached to a belt of baler twine around the waist. The top of the net was secured first at the right height on the stake to make the netting taut when the bottom was tied. Tying the tops was not too bad but having to kneel down and tie the bottom strand, with one foot on the wire to hold it down, was another story. To keep the wet mud away, we tied pieces of plastic fertilizer bags round our knees. We couldn't use the waterproof trousers as the wire and the stakes soon ripped them to bits. Fertilizer bags were for free too.

So, picture now what we actually looked like doing this job. Always a hat on your head; there are more blood vessels per square inch of skin on the scalp than any other part of the body I am told and therefore, more blood to get cold. So, cover it up and keep warm. Next a large overcoat or duffle coat. The ex-Army khaki greatcoats were a marvellous invention except, the wetter they got the heavier they became to the point where it was difficult to walk. This was on top of jerseys according to taste and the temperature. Lower down, the overall covering long trousers with bits of white or yellow fertilizer bag around each knee tied up with bits of orange baler twine. Then a pair of Wellington boots and finally the orange hank of baler tying twines hanging from a belt. If it hadn't been so serious, so practical and so necessary I would have died with laughing if I could have seen myself in a mirror.

We always took our greatcoats with us, even on seemingly fine days. There is an old Yorkshire saying that goes, "Alus teck tha coit with thee when it's fine; please tha sen when it's raining".It was remarkable how many times the weather could change in a day in early winter. It was possible to have at least three seasons before lunch time!

There was an art to tying the twine too. It had to be taken down, remember, so it was always tied using two turns and a half bow knot. This way one tail could be pulled and it could be undone quickly. When satisfied that it was all tied up, taut and strong, then bring on the dancing sheep!

Their first reaction was to get their heads down and eat off the tops of the roots. What a happy and contented sight they looked, where sheep may safely graze and all that lovely pastoral feeling. This euphoria didn't last long, normally as long as it took for them to fill their bellies. Other animals at this juncture would lie down, go to sleep and digest this enormous meal. Not our mountain lambs. Having eaten, their next consideration was how to get out of this penned up environment. The answer to a mountain lamb is simple. The biggest and strongest lamb tries to jump the fence. It couldn't quite clear it but managed to break the fence down to a low enough level so that all the others could jump it. Quite often the first lamb would get its foot stuck in the top of the netting and, being suitably snared, would wriggle and kick until either the fence came down or its foot came out.

This habit reminded me of those war films you see where the troops are going through enemy lines which are protected with barbed wire. The first trooper takes a flying leap and prostrates himself on the top of the wire. His mates then walk all over him and charge through the gap he has created with blood curdling yells and screams. Sheep do the same thing, bleating and baa-ing away. The trooper usually got a medal, the lamb the butchers knife. (Is that where Medal-lion of lamb comes from?)

Once over the fence, these pot bellied lambs would proceed to eat as many turnip tops as possible again. What was wrong with the ones still left in their own fenced off bit? Now after this has happened a couple of times, a good shepherd will be able to identify the ring leader and constant first leaper of the flock. We used to keep a stock of old bottomless metal and plastic buckets for this purpose. The "baddy" would be captured by the sheriff and a posse of men and the bucket slipped over its head, bottom towards its shoulders. The lamb could still eat through the open end but it sure stopped it from jumping. Then there were those who tried to get smart, usually the smaller ones. They knew they couldn't jump the fence so they would get their noses under the bottom wire and push their way through. Their thickening fleeces gave them plenty of anti wire-scratching protection along their backs. These little devils were scuppered, if you could catch them, by tying a short stake around their necks as bits of stake were in more plentiful supply than old buckets.

After that particular ration of roots had been eaten down, and by down, I mean that the roots had been nibbled away to below ground level, then it was time to move the fence. This act, in theory, sounds easy. Just a repeat performance of putting it up the first time. The big difference is that, this time you have got sheep in the field while doing the job.

To put it up again, you first have to take it down, a roll of wire at a time. Undo all the baler twine, pull out the stakes, throw them into the row where you want to go to next and roll up the wire. Trying to drag the wire over the turnip tops is a very frustrating exercise as the mesh gets ensnared on the root tops every two feet and, having un-snagged it there, it promptly gets snagged up again somewhere else. It was easier to roll the wire up, move it and unroll it again. Where are the lambs, you will now be saying, while this is going on? Trying to break out of their prison through the gap you have created in the fence.

This is where a good dog was worth its weight in gold. The dog would patrol the gap and it would be a very brave, stupid or hungry lamb who would attempt to penetrate such a defence. Of course it wasn't absolutely foolproof though. Some budding Major-General in the lamb army would direct his troops so that one platoon made a feint attack at the fence knowing that the dog would repulse them. While this was going on the second attack group would go to the other end of the gap, some fifty yards away and certainly, several of them would get through before the dog cavalry went charging up the rows to block the breached line. Now the dog has got a big problem. Lambs on the wrong side of the fence and others still trying to make a break for it. A good dog wouldn't dither about but would cut its losses and get straight after the escapees. Its canine logic told it that if it could get around the escapees and turn them back towards where they should be, they would probably run into the next wave of their own lamb troops. These late comers, seeing their comrades now beating a very hasty retreat, with the dog nipping the heels or hanging onto the tail of the last lamb in the line, would capitulate and make a run back for their own lines. The men were not much use to the dog really at this point, as their priority task was to get the blasted fence re-erected as quickly as possible.

At the end of a day of moving sheep fences, it was a toss up as to who had the best nights' sleep, the men, the sheep or the dog. Those shepherds and sheep farmers on the hill were smart blighters. They certainly didn't want all this fuss and bother so sell the damned lambs to us lowland suckers! Despite all this palaver, the lambs would steadily put on weight. Now it was a question of when to sell them. The food supply was going to come to an end sometime and you wanted to get the last lot of lambs off to market before that happened. If you sent them off too early, then you had thrown away the profit opportunity of extra pounds of meat and were left with half a field of swedes and nothing to eat them. If you hung on to the majority of them until as late as possible, you risked running out of food for them and there was no profit margin left after buying in food. Also this could mean dumping a lot of lambs on the market and driving the price down, talk about shooting yourself in the foot. A second consideration was what was happening in the market place. If you had lambs to sell there was an excellent chance that every other farmer in the district was selling too and the old law of supply and demand would drop the price.

To me, fresh lamb and frozen lamb have a different taste, fresh, in my humble opinion, being far superior to frozen. My opinion was supported by a vast number of other people and so the butchers only purchased what they knew they could get rid of without having to freeze too much. What time of the year was it and what, in the way of public holidays and feast days, were coming up? Nearer Christmas, a large section of the population have a tendency towards peace on earth and goodwill to all men especially those who they don't want to have around for a meal at Christmas, so they invite them for dinner before the feast day. The thought of the forthcoming superabundance of turkey, chicken and ham, subconsciously seems to drive the housewife towards something else at this time of the year. And what better than a bit of nice juicy lamb with mint sauce, blackberry and apple jelly from the autumn, berry picking, Sunday sessions. With some new potatoes, if you can still find a few, and sweet little garden peas, you have a meal fit for a king and all his subjects.

This pursuit of haute cuisine meant that we had the job every Monday morning, first light, of fetching the sheep in to the handling and sorting pens and by eye and feel of their backs and fat tails, select a parcel of lambs for the slaughter. These we would normally take to market in our own small cattle trailer which also had a second deck for sheep. As fifteen fat lambs was about enough for one load, it was not uncommon for us to make two journeys to the market some twenty miles away, before the sales started at ten o'clock. The traffic policemen didn't care if you missed the market or not, that was no excuse for speeding. The later you were, the more chance there was of a hold up at the off-loading bays as everybody had the same problem trying to get their animals selected and off to market. A long time ago, the selling order of the livestock used to be in the same order as it arrived at the market. This caused tremendous traffic congestion in our market town, its one way traffic system brought about by the fact that the Romans didn't have the foresight to build wider streets. They built them pretty straight but certainly not big enough for farmers in a hurry, driving a Landrover pulling a trailer. The system was then changed to a far more equitable method whereby the lots were all numbered and the starting sale was determined by drawing a number out of a hat like a raffle. The sale started with that number and went through to the last number before starting at number one again.

You could never guess where the better prices would be bid, at the beginning or end of the sale. The butcher knew how many head he wanted to buy and sometimes, if the other butchers were a bit late, he could pick up the first few pens for a song. At the other end of the sale, depending on the demand, the price could go up if a few butchers suddenly realised that they hadn't bought their full requirements and there were only a few lots still left to go under the hammer. Alternatively, enough was enough for the butcher unless the price dropped.

We split the day's batch of lambs into pens of three, four or maximum five on the grounds that there were very few butchers who wanted, say, ten lambs at one go. A butcher wouldn't necessarily want to buy all his lambs from one supplier either, just in case they weren't as good as they looked to be. It was important to put four lambs of the same sort of weight and condition together as the price being called by the auctioneer was the price per animal. If you mixed a little one in with three big ones you could bet the price of the pen would drop as the butcher had already worked out that the little one wasn't worth it. The same effect was experienced if you put one big one into a pen of three little ones. This time the farmer didn't get the right price for the big one and the butcher thought he had got a real bargain lot. Selling lambs was always a tricky business and you went home either unhappy, or not as happy as you could have been. It was a constant process of learning and change.

Lambs from our own breeding flock were typically marketed long before the bought-in mountain lambs. It was always a close race to get some of them fat enough for the Easter market, a traditional time for lamb to appear on the menu. What made it more difficult was that Easter is not a fixed date festival and can vary from early to late by several weeks. In just a few weeks, lambs can grow, from too small to even bother slaughtering, to a very nice shoulder or leg size. It also depended very much on what the early Spring weather was like and had the new grass, high in protein, begun to grow? You could finish them on an expensive concentrated food but the economics didn't usually allow this. Also, working backwards, when were the ewes put to the ram?

Tupping time, as it was called, had to commence when the ewes were sufficiently rested from their previous crop of lambs. The gestation period of sheep is almost five months, give or take a day or so. One ram can service anywhere from forty to sixty ewes over a period of time. It can take him up to six weeks to get around his harem at the end of which time, he is ready for a good rest. He gets it then for the next ten and a half months. Fancy having a job like that, work yourself almost to death, pleasurably too, for six weeks and then loaf for the rest of the year!

The ewe will come into heat as the days start to shorten, which, in Yorkshire, is any time from July onwards. Adding five months to this date means lambs start to drop from the end of November onwards. The ewe stays in season for only about twenty seven hours and, if she is not serviced within this time, then she will come in season again after sixteen days. To find out those that have been serviced, the ram is fitted with a harness holding a special marking dye. As he mounts the ewe the dye is transferred on to her back. If the colour of the dye is changed every sixteen days it is easy to see which ewes didn't conceive on the first service. If they have three or four different colours on them at the end of the tupping season, it would be a fair bet that she was barren and would be culled from the flock, fattened and sold for mutton. To avoid cries of "sexist" from the women's lib group, yes, it could also be the ram who was infertile. If all his ewes returned for service it was a certainty that the blame would rest firmly at the ram's door. He would be rapidly substituted too for not scoring. It was always preferable, to avoid this happening to use two or three rams together on the same flock. This could result in some very fierce fighting between the rams to the extent that the ewes wouldn't get serviced. It was always very difficult to know if the rams would spend their time fighting or doing what was expected of them.

All the rams were kept together during their resting period in the same small paddock. They had to be kept lean until shortly before mating season when they would be readied for their duties with extra rations to get them fit. During this period they would sort out the pecking order of who was the senior amongst them, the biggest usually winning too. If he was far superior to his mates, no problem. If they were fairly evenly matched then the fights would occur as soon as they were introduced to the females. Does that sound fairly familiar in a human context too? The difference being that the poor old ewe isn't given a say in who her suitor will be.

After the ewes had got rid of their previous crop of lambs, it was time to give them a holiday rest period too. This was done by putting them on a poor pasture initially to prevent them from getting too fat. About two weeks before tupping time they would be given the very best of food available on the farm. New grass, if planted from seed, was the first choice or a diet of edible rape and a concentrated food with plenty of oats in it. They would start to bloom and improve in condition very rapidly. This process was called "flushing" and was a prerequisite for high fertility rates. As we had a good supply of food available for the ewes in winter, we could afford to allow the ewes to have twins or triplets. The farmers on the moors didn't really encourage this as they knew that their pastures would not give sufficient nutrition for a feeding ewe to support two lambs. The lambing percentage is always a bragging point among farmers in the pubs. If you could hit an average of two lambs per ewe you were doing very well indeed. To hit this target you had to get everything just right and have a lot of luck too, with the weather. In particular, we always found that the earlier in the mating season they fell pregnant, the more chance there was of the ewe throwing twins or triplets. The more lambs the better remember, that's what it's all about in the end.

Before they lambed, the ewes were given a bit of extra food to keep them fit to help them produce the much needed milk. We used to let the ewes lamb in the fields, keeping a close watch on them at this time. It could be an exhausting time too as it involved getting up several times during the night from a warm bed, getting dressed and going out in to a cold and usually damp, dark winter night. It seemed in lambing time that you had no sooner gone back to bed when the alarm clock would go off and away you went again. A nap after lunch certainly helped even if it was only half an hour. This went on for about six weeks in all.

We felt it best not to interfere with Mother Nature unless absolutely vital. Most of the time the ewes would sort their own lives out and produce their offspring without any bother at all. Then there were the other times. We feared most of all a wet lambing season of cold, incessant rain. Lambs are generally hardy little creatures at birth and could stand sub zero temperatures and snow by getting under Mum as quickly as possible. That was where the food bar was too so what a sensible place to go. When it was wet the newly born lambs didn't get a chance to warm up at all. Many a lamb has had to be taken into the kitchen in the house and put close to the fire for a few hours. If you took the lambs you also took the ewe too. A good mother would want to chase you away from her lambs in her attempts to protect them from all harm. This could work to your advantage as, if you picked up the lambs and walked away with them, she would follow you. We used to tie straw bales together to make small pens if the field was distant from the farm buildings. If close to the farm, we could usually find some covered area to give them a couple of days relief from the weather and then heartlessly push them back out into the cold fields. By then they would be quite happy to get out. In very bad weather the ewes would instinctively look to find some shelter, normally a hedgerow on the lee side of the wind. This was fine until, in their pre-natal prancing and circling, they would get tangled up with the hedge. Such hedges therefore had to be patrolled at frequent intervals during the night, on foot armed with a torch and a shepherd's crook with which to catch the ewe.

Sometimes a ewe would have trouble with the birth and had to be helped. If she was carrying twins, they may have been racing to get out and got jammed together. That was quite an easy operation, push one back in and tell it to wait, and help the first one out. The second usually followed of its own free will. If she was having a single lamb, it might be too big for her to manage so, again, assistance was required. If she was having three lambs she would often forget where one of the lambs had been dropped and then it was a question of trying to re-unite mother and abandoned child as quickly as possible. We had, very infrequently, thank goodness, to perform a caesarian section on the ewe there and then in the field. I say thank goodness because it was a messy, bloody affair and frequently, the result was that you lost the ewe or the lambs or both. The operation was done with a pocket knife and a needle and cotton. If there was time, and he was available at short notice, the vet could be called out to do it. His chances of success were considerably better than ours but, because of the conditions in the field, not always a certainty either. It was preferable to get the ewe into a warm, dry straw filled or concrete floored box if you had time.

If a lamb died, especially a single lamb, we had to do some surreptitious "family" shuffling about. The ewe knew, by smell, which was her lamb alright. Sometimes other lambs would get the wrong mother and try to suckle her. The lamb would be very smartly seen off with a fierce butt of the head. To fool the mother, we would select a very recently born lamb of a twin or a triplet family. The dead lamb would be skinned and the skin wrapped around the selected lamb so that it carried her own lamb's scent. Nine times out of ten the mother would be fooled totally and accept the lamb without a problem. It also helped to rub the mother's nose in anything with a lingering and distracting scent, say, a good pine disinfectant. This would just upset her sense of smell long enough for her not to examine the foster lamb too closely. If the lamb and foster mother were penned up together for a few hours, that helped too. How to fool sheep! It also proved to me, very conclusively, that animal recognition was all done by smell at that very early age. Later on, when the lambs grew a little more adventurous and would get together with other lambs to frolic and gambol around, at the first sign of danger, say the dog arriving in the field, the mother would call to the lamb which would home in on the sound. She would always nuzzle it and have a sniff at it to make sure she had the right one.

On occasions, we wound up with a lamb whose mother had either died, rejected it or lost its milk. Then somebody had the task of hand rearing the lamb. Having pet lambs, as they were called, is a romantic and supremely pastoral thing that Little Bo-Peep stories are made up from. Pet lambs can be a decided nuisance and an unwanted chore. At a very early age they have to be fed at almost hourly intervals with specially warmed milk from a baby's bottle. They then fall into the same habits as babies and cry loudly if they are hungry, a physical happening seemingly every thirty minutes. It is fairly natural to hold the lamb and feed it and this gives the lamb a very strong sense of comfort and familiarity towards the regular feeder. So much so that who ever was feeding the lambs was constantly followed around by them.

We made the mistake of hand rearing one lamb and, as its pen was a bit too far away on a wet day, letting it stay in the back kitchen with the dogs. The dogs didn't seem to mind this at all and the lamb thought it was a fine arrangement and would cuddle up next to the dog out of choice to sleep at night. The trouble was that, after a while, the lamb thought it was a dog and would start to bleat every time the dogs started to bark. It would then go outside with the dogs to do its business and would scratch at the door with its tiny hooves to be let back in again. It followed its feeder, usually the lady of the house, throughout the house, yes! even to the loo! If allowed to, it would make itself at home, curled up in front of the hearth. Then, to demand food it started to jump up at the lady, would ladder several pairs of tights and be eventually banished back to a pen of its own before being re-introduced to the paddocks.

One evening we had some people around for dinner and the lamb was, naughtily and surreptitiously, fed some beer by one of the guests. The result was absolutely hilarious. The poor little creature got severely pickled on a small quantity of beer and entertained the gathering with funny little dashes and charges around the room on very wobbly legs. It eventually ran out of fuel and collapsed in a heap in front of the fire and slept soundly until morning.

The heartbreak to a family of keeping a pet lamb was having to eventually get rid of it back to the field. Nobody spoke to anybody else when this happened, and for several days, the house seemed strangely deserted and quiet. Having lived with, and slept with, the dogs, the first thing that happened when you entered the field with the dog was that your ex-pet lamb would go running up to the dog to greet it like a long lost pal. The dog didn't quite know what to make of this unruly animal who was totally ignoring canine authority by being over familiar in front of the rest of the flock. This animal didn't run away from a dog as it should but ran towards it! How confusing.

Young lambs also required "doctoring". Handling them was at least a little less strenuous than having to tip their huge mothers onto their backsides, that was, of course, after you had caught them. The little devils can run and jump better than a bunch of Olympic hurdlers! A great deal of consternation was also evident amongst the matronly Mama's who took umbrage at their off spring being handled by human beings and protested very loudly. Some of the more determined and protective mothers would actually charge and if butted in the delicate part of one's anatomy, could really bring tears to a grown man's eyes! In the real "way back when" days, the young male lambs were castrated using a sharp knife. Some of the old shepherds from the hills used their teeth, after the initial cut, to sever the cord. These sweetbreads were considered a shepherds culinary delicacy when cooked with onions and a few herbs. In later years the use of a small elastic band was considered to be far more hygienic and had less risk of infection than an open cut. The Elastrator, as it was called, was a fairly thick rubber ring which was applied using a metal gadget which opened the ring wide enough to slip it on. We used this method for castration and also for tail docking. Now, before anybody starts on about the cruelty aspect of tail docking, let's just look at a few very good reasons for doing it.

Firstly, as this area of the sheep is prone to becoming wet and damp, it provided a perfect place for flies to lay their eggs. As the eggs hatched out, the resulting maggots would eat their way into the sheep and make a very painful and debilitating mess of the whole back end of the animal. Secondly, if the sheep were to be fed on cultivated crops, such as swedes in winter, the tail would become totally clogged with mud and very heavy. Because it was heavy the sheep couldn't lift its tail high enough when it wanted to go to the loo. This resulted in the faecal matter sticking to the tail and effectively, gluing the tail to the legs. When this happened, the poor sheep couldn't pass faeces as it couldn't get it out and so, the animal became sort of constipated. Finally, if the lambs were going to be used for breeding, the long and thick tail became a very good substitute for a chastity belt and the ewe considered infertile and finished up a mutton stew. All this because it had a tail!

The action of the Elastrator band, although painful for a short while after application, was a very foolproof and clean way of solving these problems. The band was placed at the top of the scrotum, ensuring that both testicles were inside the pouch. Little lambs, especially on a cold day can retract their testicles back into their belly and when you thought you had castrated the lot, were later amazed to find so many young female lambs getting pregnant. At the same time, the tail was docked by applying another Elastrator ring around the top of the tail. When the lamb was released their leaping and cavorting took on new and interesting patterns around the field as they tried in vain to get these painful attachments off. After about an hour the area obviously became numb and the lambs settled down to normal routine. As soon as they were released from this human torture, they would gallop around looking for mother, bleating away. Mother was also galloping around looking for junior so you can imagine the noise and confusion that reigned. Within a few weeks, the appendages started to drop off and would litter the fields and pastures for a while, if they hadn't been picked up as a delicacy by the local fox or vixen who had their own cubs to feed at about this time of the year.

Living fairly close to a small town, the towns-folk would consider it their right to take their dogs out into the country for a gallop around. This was a weekend habit mainly. On arriving at the parking spot of their choice, they would unthinkingly let their dogs off the leash. Now there is something about a flock of sheep that excites a dog; the sheep become totally irresistible play things to be chased around. Oh, what fun to see these funny woolly creatures gallop around in a mad panic stricken way. If the sheep were in lamb, it was a dead certainty that several ewes would abort their lambs after such a chasing. The dog was usually, by now, quite uncontrollable and could not be captured. The procedure was to fetch the shotgun, shoot the dog and have a tremendous argument afterward with the bereaved dog owner. Then we would go about suing the dog owner for damages, a drawn out affair unless they coughed up out of court. Sounds very nasty, but what else could you do? It's a great pity that the magistrate didn't sentence the dog owner to several months of farming community work with sheep. Education may have been a better way out.

Packs of dogs, from who knows where, would suddenly appear, especially at lambing time. It was then a case of shoot as many as you could, hand the carcasses over to the police and let them sort out the owners. Carrion crows were an occasional pest too. They would do a fairly good job of disposing of the afterbirths from the lambing which otherwise would have attracted foxes. If the crows were a bit hungry, they could get carried away and would easily peck the eyes out of a newly born lamb, killing it in the process. So with all these natural and unnatural predators, weather, dogs, crows and foxes it was a wonder that we had any lambs left at all!

A good sheepdog is worth four men most of the time. To the moorland farmers, a dog was quite often all the staff the farmer employed. The Income Tax man even recognised that a dog was essential on a farm and used to give an allowance for its care and maintenance too. The dog was the only thing that could get into some of the nooks and crannies around the crags and fells.

Training sheepdogs is an art and a skill, requiring a considerable amount of time and patience. The first hurdle to overcome was to select a pup from good working dogs. Somebody always knew who had good dogs, but they didn't come cheap, quality rarely does. If the pup came from a "town" dog it could have lost some of its natural instincts. We always used Border Collies and, for some unknown reason, always picked one with a bit of brown colour among the black and white. I can't tell you why, but somehow, it seems to "soften" the dog's features.

A good size of dog was important too as a small dog can be intimidated by a matronly ewe. The coats of these dogs, especially in winter become long and rather shaggy and they have "feathers" of hair growing on the rear side of their legs. These "feathers" soon became a nuisance when working with the sheep in winter on ploughed fields with root crops. The wet mud would stick to the hair and dry out into beads of rock hard consistency. These beads would clatter and clang as the dogs walked. Because of this they were never allowed into a carpeted room for obvious reasons! They always slept on sacks filled with soft hay in the back kitchen of the house and seemed as happy as Larry there.

The dogs were frequently one man dogs and, anybody else, other than the regular handler, would invariably have a communication problem with them. The old shepherd used to wait until the dogs were big enough, say eight months old, and then tie the young dog to an old, trained dog. The old dog knew what it had to do at each different whistled command or shout and it wasn't very long before the young dog stopped bucking and dragging and went along with the old dog. It must still be exhausting for the old dog though, having to drag a youngster around all day. It also slowed down the work rate too as the old dog, wanting to go in the commanded direction, could be literally sidetracked by the youngster wanting to chase something else. Before this stage the young dog had to learn the basics, sit, lie down, stay, come, heel, stop. This was done using an ever increasingly long piece of twine attached to the dog's training collar. I can't ever remember one of our dogs being beaten or whipped. When they were pups, and made their mess in the back kitchen, their noses were rubbed in it and they were shown the door. They soon learnt that outside was the place for that function! As soon as they had a few manners, they would accompany the owner all the time, all day, everywhere. They would soon learn how to jump inside a car without standing on the seats and would lie where passengers would put their feet. They also went on the tractors and would lie all day on the foot board alongside the driver's seat where it was warm. When we got around to tractors with cabs on them it was a mighty leap for them to get in but they did. Open the door, whistle and in they would jump. It was safer for them to be in the cab than run alongside the tractor.

By law in England, dogs had to wear a collar. This law did not apply to farm and sheepdogs as there was a real danger of the collar snagging in a hedge and strangling the dog. The only time our dogs wore a collar was for training or, if we had a bitch on heat, to keep her in a safe place. The lack of a collar made it difficult sometimes, as the dogs would get into fights if their territory was invaded and then it was a case of grabbing them by the scruff of the neck and pulling! We once lost a good dog when visiting somebody else's farm. The dog jumped out of the car and had a serious tussle with two local dogs. Our dog ran away and refused to come back. It disappeared for two days but then was seen early in the morning around the farm buildings. When the local farmer tried to catch it, it ran off again. The following day, I had to spend the night at this farm and getting up at dawn, hung around the buildings whistling at frequent intervals. Within a quarter of an hour the dog appeared from seemingly nowhere, much to my joy, and you should have seen how happy the dog was. It was thin, having missed its food for three days but couldn't stop wriggling with joy and smiling at me and making funny, happy, noises. Those who have dogs will know just how a dog can smile when it's happy. It jumped into the car with glee and we smiled and chatted all the way home where he was totally spoiled for the rest of the day by the delighted household.

Dogs were not allowed into our local pub. The exception was mine as it would come slinking in behind me, knowing that it was there under sufferance of the landlord, and would lie still and quiet as a mouse under the bench seat of the snug bar. Others would try to coax it to come out but it stayed put until it was time to go. Nobody was allowed to feed it bit of potato crisps or peanuts and if they did, with one word, "No", it would let the food lie there all night if it wasn't removed. One eye would watch the food and the other would be watching me for any sign of generosity.

We had some chickens which were free range birds. They spent all their relatively short lives out in the paddock in wooden chicken huts. Their access to the hut was through a "bob" hole, as we called it low down near the floor. The birds always used to put themselves to bed at night, just before dusk. Now in Europe, dusk in summer can be as late as ten o'clock at night and after a hard day that was long after my bedtime. The only way to get the chickens into the "bob" hole was to herd them in there. The fowl would get close to the hole and then decide not to go in. It was hilarious watching the sheepdogs, working as a team, put the chickens to bed. The dogs would gently and slowly round them up and when one chicken went around the corner of the hut, the dog would race round the hut the other way to stand and meet the chicken on its way round. The chicken would turn tail and head back and the dog would shoot around the hut again to stop it from going past the "bob" This tearing around the hut would continue until the last one was in, and the sliding drop door covering the hole could be dropped into place for the night. Such was the value of a good sheep dog to us. It does rather pain me to see Border Collies being kept as domestic pets in towns and cities. They need freedom and a place to put their natural instincts to work. They are not lap dogs like other breeds are.

You can't have sheep without a dog or two, it's just too much running around for an average person. Sheep are not particularly intelligent animals at all and you need all the help you can get with them. While most of our dogs were good, hard working, intelligent, incredibly loyal animals, we also had our failures. We had a pair of pups called Ike and Mike. Ike was a slim, super intelligent dog, more brown than any other colour. He was keen, sharp and very quick to learn. He was however, a little bit reserved and didn't want too much of a fuss made of him. It seemed to embarrass him. Mike was exactly the opposite. He was black and white and a very big dog, much bigger than his brother, more like his father. He was also greedy and would eat his food, Ike's food, old Shep's food and the cat's too before you could blink. He only "sort of" tried to be a sheep dog and generally caused havoc as he was virtually out of control the moment he stepped into a field. He was loveable though, as faithful as any dog could be, loved all the attention that was lavished on him because his brother would keep his distance. He was too nice a dog to get rid of so we kept him, at home! He made an excellent guard dog and the local reps would not get out of their cars until Mike had been told that they were decent and welcome human beings. As a watchdog we had him to thank for saving the farm.

One night, Mike started barking and, knowing that he didn't bark without reason, we got up and looked out through the bedroom window. The sky was lit up with a reddish light towards the Dutch barnyard area. The barn was on fire! Having phoned the Fire Brigade, who were on the scene within five minutes, we galloped down to the barnyard and tried to move what we could. We lost a lot of the straw and hay but at least were able to save some of the valuable machinery like the combine harvester which was parked there. Every dog has his day, they say, and that was Mike's.

Chapter 6

Cereal Crops

English school holidays always seemed to coincide with some of the busiest periods of the farming calendar. I think the Minister of Education in those days had a farm of his own and therefore understood the necessity of having a large number of enthusiastic, energetic and naughty school kids around to take all the hard work of farming onto their spiny backs. The Easter holiday tended to coincide with the planting of Spring corn and weeding root crops, the summer holiday with haymaking and corn harvesting, the October half term holiday with potato lifting and the Christmas holiday with potato sorting and relief work when the regular staff were given a break.

Of all these school holiday times, my favourite was harvest. Like most English mixed farms, we grew quite a lot of cereal crops, and for a variety of reasons too. Pigs thrive on a home made food mixture, the basic ingredient being barley. Barley and oats had to be sown in the springtime, as soon as the land could be worked. The straw of both these crops was also fairly palatable and so cattle would eat it with relish. We also used barley for cattle food when mixed with flaked maize, linseed oil cake, groundnut oil cake, soya bean meal, fish meal, sugar beet pulp, vitamins and minerals, bran and what ever else was available in the way of food by-products. The grain was ground to a rough powder, using our own grinding mill, and these various additives were used to make it more nutritious and more palatable. The mixing was done, by hand, on the chamber floor, using the biggest shovels we could find as the material was fairly light in weight. It would then be bagged and taken to the animals. Depending on the quality of the barley we could sometimes sell it for malting purposes for the brewing of beer.

Oats was always used as the last crop in the cereal rotation as the demands on soil fertility were considerably lower than other cereals. If a crop of oats was grown on highly fertile soil, it would lodge so badly that it would be almost impossible to harvest. Oat straw is generally longer in length than that of wheat or barley and would fall down and lie flat with a single puff of wind. Oats were also used for feeding, especially the horses and for cattle too. If you want to know which cereal gives you the most energy and strength, ask a Scotsman!

Wheat was generally planted in the late autumn, especially after a crop of potatoes, grass or a leguminous crop such as beans and peas. Following these crops gave the high nitrogen needed, and the generally high residual fertility these crops left in the soil. The wheat would grow to about eight inches high before the cold of the winter forced the plant to hibernate for a while. All cereal crops "tiller". That means that if you plant one seed, up to twenty or more shoots would grow from it. Cold weather encouraged these shoots to form with wheat and the plant could stand being frosted whereas, barley and oats would die from frost burn.

Another way to encourage the wheat to tiller was to let the sheep graze it lightly in the spring. Like mowing a lawn, the harder they ate it down, the more tillers were produced. Our wheat was always sold to the millers for feed. Wheat for bread has to be a very hard grained variety, high in gluten. The gluten in the wheat makes the dough rubbery and quite tough so that it traps the carbon dioxide formed by the yeast. It's this trapped gas which makes the bread dough light when cooked and gives the baker more loaves for his bag of grain. Being difficult to grow in England, most hard milling wheat is imported from places like Canada, America and Australia. The hardest wheat grown in England was only just suitable for cake and biscuit flour really. The rest of the wheat used to be made into, mainly, chicken food as it was easier for chickens to digest it. Feeding wheat to other livestock was not really an economical proposition as the yield of wheat was lower per acre than that of barley and oats. Big advances in plant breeding have now produced varieties of all the cereals that can safely be planted in autumn. The longer the plant can spend in the field the higher the eventual yield.

Though harvest time was a pleasant time, it also had some drawbacks too. In the days before combined harvesters were widely used, all the corn was cut with a binder. The corn was tested for maturity with the teeth. If the grain was dry and mature enough to harvest, it would crack into two as you bit it. We would wander through the fields, me up to my chest in corn, pulling off ears of wheat here and there, threshing it by rubbing the ear between your hands, blowing away the chaff and biting the grain. A serious opinion which, at that age, was totally ignored, was then passed. When it was cracking nicely, the adults would say, "Aye, she'll go" and wander back to get the machinery going. As the sheepdogs always accompanied us on such field visits, I have a memory of getting very concerned that the dogs would get lost in the field. The dogs were having a marvellous time though as the fields were riddled with rabbits and hares. A canine paradise! The dogs would keep a watchful eye on us by jumping up into the air, above the corn height, at frequent intervals to see where we had got to.

Back at the farm, the binders, all ready for the harvest season having been serviced and worked on during the preceding weeks, were rolled out. We had horse drawn binders at first, each machine pulled by

two great Shire horses. The binder mechanism was driven by a large steel wheel with big lugs on it, which, when pulled forward, transferred power via an assortment of chains, to the various vital parts. The first of such parts was the cutting knife. This deadly looking weapon consisted of a flat steel bar, about eight feet long onto which were riveted many small, sharpened triangular blades. As the machine was pulled forward the knife moved back and forth between steel fingers which also acted as guides and the corn stalk was duly cut. The corn then fell onto the table, a continuous canvas belt with wooden lathes riveted to it, which travelled sideways to the direction the binder was moving in. To assist the knives and to help drop the corn onto the table, a set of slow moving flails, like windmill sails, rotated through the crop at a pre-set speed. These sails also held the corn stalk against the moving knife to assist the cutting action. The corn then disappeared into the bowels of the machine which contained the knotting mechanism. The sheaf, now tied in the centre with sisal twine was then ejected from the machine by a set of metal fingers which were strong enough to throw the sheaf well away from the machine. All this activity was controlled by a man sitting fairly high up on a metal seat, giving him a fine view of the canvas bed and the sheaves being ejected. He could, through a series of long handled levers, vary the height at which the corn was cut at and the height and aggressiveness setting of the sails. At the same time, the horses had to be controlled too, a good job for a small boy sitting on the back of the left hand horse so that the cutting edge was visible to him. The first hour of this work was exciting, the second hour was tedious and

thereafter it was sheer boredom, complete with, by now, a very painful and stiff backside. The operator had plenty to do. The corn would get jammed up against the knives and the cutter bar had to be cleared, the machine suddenly decided not to tie the sheaves and so the knotter mechanism had to be adjusted. Stones would jam between the pick up fingers, sometimes breaking sections of the knife. Every time the machine was stopped and the operator got off, he was able to stretch his legs. As the driver, I was too small to climb onto the horses' back on my own and had to be unceremoniously thrown up, sometimes slipping and falling down again between the two horses, scrambling out from underneath them on hands and knees and being thrown up again with sharp words to "hang on to 'im" from the operator.

The highlight of the work was the hot tea, sandwiches and cream cakes that seemed to appear at regular intervals through the day, to be eaten sitting on a freshly cut sheaf of corn in the shade of a hedgerow tree. The tea was usually brought by another man who also brought a fresh pair of horses and he would unhitch the tired pair and couple up the fresh pair. Tea time was over as soon as he had finished this changeover task as there was never a moment to lose during harvest time. You never knew when the weather was going to change to rain and you cannot cut wet corn, the stalks go soft and the knife just won't cut it cleanly. In some years, when the ground underfoot was damp, the big drive wheel would skid along the ground instead of biting and driving. This caused a series of reactions, all costing precious time. As all mechanical force through the drive mechanism was lost as soon as the wheel stopped, the cutter bar would jam up with corn stalks and invariably, due to the excessive force, the drive chains would break. Although the chains were specifically designed for easy and speedy repair it was still a nuisance which brought plenty of vitriolic comment from the operator.

To avoid the horses trampling down the first swathe around the field, a pathway was cut out by hand some days before the binder went in. This was done by a gang of men with scythes, steadily and gracefully sweeping their scythes through the corn with a ballet-like rhythm. The corn was then collected into sheaves and a tying rope made by twisting together handfuls of corn stalks to bind these sheaves. This was the way that fields of corn used to be harvested before binders were invented. Each scythe operator had a sharpening stone in his back pocket and, as a way of having a breather from the swinging action, the scythe would be up-ended onto its handle and the blade stroked with the sharpening stone until the operator was satisfied or had recovered enough to carry on.

Swinging a scythe looks easy but, like many other actions which look easy in experienced hands, it is in fact an art, which takes a lot of practice. The muscles used are not the ones you use every day either as the arms are brought from right to left across the body and back. Cutting the corn, instead of pulling it out of the ground with the blade, means

that the angle the scythe is taken through the standing corn has to be pretty exact. The shallower the angle the easier it cuts but one's natural inclination is to try to take too large a bite at a time with the blade too far open. Then you have to fiddle and chop at the tangled mess you have made. A scythe is also a dangerous piece of equipment and can chop a man's leg very badly. For this reason a wide space is always given between two scythe operators and the followers tying up the sheaves.

Once the field had been opened out and the horses could get around the perimeter of the field, the cutting started in earnest. Round and round you go at a steady plodding pace, the ejector fingers banging out sheaves about every five seconds. At the corners of the field, the easiest way to turn the ninety degrees left was to make a wide circle to the right. This meant that you were lined up to the face edge of the corn before you started cutting again. This is where the horseman came into his own as he had to judge the circular turn exactly right and also turn with a wide enough radius to prevent damage to the binder. As there were always sheaves dropped right in the turning area, a couple of men were always tasked with removing these offending sheaves from the corners, each man taking two corners of the field. At the end of the day, these men must have walked miles from one corner to the next and back again to keep pace with the binder. As evening approached, you could see the strip of standing corn getting narrower and narrower and you played mental guessing games with yourself trying to work out how many more times you had to go round before the field was finished and would you beat the darkness that was falling.

As the fields were very rarely square, there was always a small piece of corn left in the centre. At this juncture, almost by magic, several good friends used to arrive armed with shotguns. The resident hares would stay inside the standing corn which was giving them protection and cover. As the binder went round and round they would congregate in the centre of the field, in the last remaining piece. Having agreed their arcs of fire, the shooters would take up their positions either side of the remaining standing corn. Without warning, a hare would bolt from this cover and head for the security of the next field, jumping with long, bounding leaps between bursts of lightning running. There would be a crack of a shotgun and the hare would tumble and roll under the force of its own momentum and then lie still in the stubble. That was always assuming that the shooter was a good enough shot. For every hare that wound up in a pot, at least five must have got away. Sometimes the hare would be panicked into running the wrong way, straight into the oncoming binder where it had a fifty- fifty chance of being decapitated in the cutting mechanism or managing to jump over, or go under, the cutter bar and table. The horses didn't always enjoy the sudden peace-shattering bang of the shotgun and would do all sorts of strange things. Some would stop dead in their tracks and stand quivering until they had been calmed down and coaxed to move again. Others were probably asleep while walking and didn't give tuppence for the noise. If you got one of each nature in a pair of horses, you could wind up going in a very small circle, pivoting about the stationary beast.

Eventually the field was cut and thousands of sheaves left scattered in orderly rows. The next urgent task was to "stook" the sheaves. "Stooking" consisted of taking six or eight rows of sheaves and making, what looked like, a small tent out of them. Two sheaves were picked up, the fingers holding the twine, and tucked one under each arm. The pair of sheaves are then brought together on the ground, corn ears uppermost, leaving a tunnel between their bases. The action was repeated until a stook of about twelve to fourteen sheaves had been constructed. The tunnel at the base allowed the wind to blow through the stook and dry the bottom of the sheaf. These little "tents" also made discreet necking spots for young lovers and hiding places for hares. Chemical weed control was still quite a way in the future and so every corn field was about half corn and half grass and weeds. Although the corn had reached maturity and had dried off, the greenery in the bottom had not. If it was put into a barn in a green condition the corn would more than likely rot, turn into something like silage or, even worse, spontaneous combustion would set the entire barn on fire. So the stooks would have to sit out in the fields for several weeks, depending on the weather conditions, before they could be taken home to the safety of the barn. This sounds rather an idyllic task, setting up stooks; it wasn't at all.

Firstly, picking up the sheaves by the twine soon made the fingers extremely sore and blistered unless gloves were worn. The corn stalks are rough and so the wrist area was scratched until bleeding. Even worse were the thistles which penetrated the skin with ease. After a day of stooking, the evening was spent with a sharp needle, digging out thistles. One old farm hand we had always used to say it was a waste of time digging them out, as it only made room for a new one to get in the next day! Thistles were bad enough but nettles were even worse, especially on the tender inner arm area. Wherever nettles grow, somewhere close will be a dock plant. The leaves of the dock plant when rubbed onto the nettle sting brings a great amount of relief from the irritation, if applied straight away. Finding the dock leaf was another problem and usually meant a walk to the hedgerow or the corner of the field. If the weather turned to rain it was all hands to the field to get it stooked before the corn rotted on the ground or started to germinate in the ear. Then the discomfort was added to by having to tuck a wet, soggy sheaf of corn under each arm, time and time again. If waterproofs were worn you got almost as wet inside as outside from the sweat produced. When corn is cut the stubble left on the ground is akin to a fakir's bed of nails. If a good pair of hobnail boots were worn, most of the problem was solved except that the stalks would go up the trouser legs, reducing the skin around the ankles and calves to a mass of scratched flesh. Wearing a pair of rubber Wellington boots was not the answer as they were too hot and uncomfortable in summer and tough stalks could penetrate them too. Even worse was the chaff and bits of corn that always found their way into the boots and under the foot part. The answer was a combination of the two. Old Wellies were never thrown away, even if the bottoms were leaking like the Titanic. By carefully cutting off the foot part, the uppers made a superb pair of leggings which would fit snugly over the laced uppers of the hobnail boots.

Having stooked all the cut corn, with the wigwams of stooks standing in silent rows until dry, the next task was to get the harvest home. We used a series of carts drawn by horses, with a gang of loaders in the field and a gang of off loaders in the barn. The barns were Dutch barns, six or eight spans of roofed-over cover space some thirty feet high. The base of the span was always covered with broken bricks and stones to act as drainage and keep the corn off the ground. Off loading was an easy job when the barn was empty as everything was thrown down hill. It was a different matter when the barn was getting full. Using long handled, two pronged, pitch forks, the sheaf was picked off the cart and hurled towards the stacker man. This sounds easy but after a while the sheaves get heavier and heavier and the stacker man was always a very particular person. His reputation stood or fell depending whether his stack stood or fell. The sheaves were laid, row at a time with the butt ends facing the outside of the barn, grain innermost. As the stacker went around the barn, he demanded that you threw the sheaf to land close to him, and pointing in the right direction, so that he didn't have to walk too far and so that he didn't have to spin every sheaf around before laying it down. This called for a certain amount of skill from the off loading fork man and even more skill from the other man on the stack called the picker. The picker was the fellow who threw the sheaf across the barn to the stacker. As the stack grew higher and higher, two pickers were needed. A small "bob" hole was left in the centre of the stack so that the off loader man could throw his sheaves into it. The first picker, perched precariously on the edge of the bob hole would then hurl the sheaf up to the second picker who, in turn, would throw it to the stacker. The stacks were taken up to the roof of the barn.

Meanwhile, back in the field, the team of loaders would drive the carts between the rows of stooks, loading from both sides simultaneously. Again a pitch fork was used, the sheaf being speared on its point of balance somewhere around the tying twine, hoisted aloft and with a turn at the top, the sheaf would be deposited on the dray or cart for the stacker to position. When the cart was getting full, and the top of the stacked cart was higher than the loader could reach, even with a five foot handle to his fork, the sheaf had to be tossed on the top. Sometimes the man tossing the sheaf would let go of the fork as well and this potentially lethal missile would end up on top of the cart. The five foot long handle often caught the stacker man unawares, always assuming that the sharp fork tines hadn't impaled him to the load. Much cursing ensued and the more often it happened, usually as the loaders got weary, the more likely it was that the stacker would use the fork like a javelin and threaten to impale the loader as it was thrown back down again. Who ever said that farming is a peaceful and pleasant occupation? Only some romantic fiction writer who has never experienced such dangers!

Once fully loaded, and each load was gauged to the condition of the cart track out of the field, the sheaves would be roped down to the cart and off it went to the barn yard. The tracks were usually in a badly rutted state from years of cart wheels travelling over them in some very wet weather. We did try to maintain the tracks by filling in the deepest potholes with rubble from torn down houses. All this did was to create humps in the ruts which caused the cart and the load to teeter precariously. It was a fairly common occurrence to have the load thrown off half way down the track which blocked the track and held up the entire operation. If the load was stacked too high, branches of overhanging trees would soon level the top of the load off. The track was not owned by the farm but was a Council responsibility and was also used by three other farmers who had land in that area. The Council never bothered to repair it, despite many strong letters to, and verbal abusing of, the local Council representative.

Unless the weather conditions were really superb, and in Yorkshire the chance of that is about one in every hundred years, the corn was always stacked and threshed at a later date. I hated threshing days. A threshing machine was a huge, cumbersome, chunk of machinery designed to produce as much dust and noise as possible. It was driven by a wide, long, flat canvas belt from a tractor pulley wheel. It used to take about two days to set it up properly as any slight mis-alignment of the tractor would cause the belt to go flying off like an angry snake, clapping and clacking, as the faces of the belt met in mid air. At the other end of the machine, where the threshed straw came out, was a batting machine. The latter, rather similar to part of the binder, caught the straw from the thresher and tied it into huge sheaves called "batts". The batts were then placed into another barn or made into a stack out in the open depending on what kind of crop was being threshed. Wheat straw is generally very unpalatable to animals and used only for bedding for cattle. Barley and oat straw is much softer and cattle seemed to relish eating it, and nutritious too. If there was a lot of green matter in the field at harvest time, the straw would be like good hay.

The threshing machine was positioned close to the stack of sheaves due to be threshed. Two men would be on the stack tossing the sheaves to the threshing machine. There, another man, armed with a special curved knife tied to his wrist, would pick up the sheaf by the twine and cut it allowing the corn laden straw to disappear into the jaws of the machine while he was left holding the cut twine. You didn't want the twine to go into the thresher as it would wrap itself around each and every rotating shaft it came into contact with, causing so much friction that threshing machines had been known to burst into flames, a sure disaster as it was surrounded by highly combustible straw and dust.

A threshing machine is a very simple machine made complicated by engineers. It consists of a rotating drum of metal which flails the sheaf, throwing the corn out of it. The grain then goes through a series of sieves which have air blown through them to separate out the chaff. The chaff is returned to the now threshed straw. The grain is also sorted by the machine, heavy grain to one end and the light pieces and weed seed, called tailings, to the other. Sacks were hung from specially provided hooks on the machine and, as they were filled, were then weighed into eight stone bags for barley and oats and ten or twelve stone bags for wheat. An eight stone bag, one hundred and twelve pounds or a hundredweight as it was known, was not too bad to hump around. The twelve stone bag of wheat, with one hundred and sixty eight pound in it, was an inhuman invention and not often used unless the Corn Merchant specifically demanded it in that sack size. The sacks, tied with the twine from the sheaves being cut into the machine, were then loaded onto a cart ready for the corn chamber.

As the corn sheaves had been sitting in the stack for several months, any fungus or dust was by now ready to escape its bondage and, it did, everywhere. After a wet harvesting time, the dust was always particularly bad, and we put wet handkerchiefs over our mouths and noses and struggled to breathe all day. This dust was notorious and was later found to be one of the major causes of Farmer's Lung, pneumonicosis, I suppose it must have been. Most old farmers we knew seemed to die of this type of emphysema, struggling painfully to draw their last breath. In those days there were no regulations and nothing like dust-proof face masks for the workers. It was a wet hankie and a good coughing and hawking session later in the day together with a solid nose picking session. Pretty disgusting but as one old chap once told me, sitting having a good old picking session, "God gave us a little finger so we could pick threshing dust out of our noses"!

At the other end of the machine, the straw was being dropped into the batting machine and several men would be carting and stacking it. If the chaff was needed as separate cattle food, it was not blown back into the straw but was collected and carried on chaff sheets, big sheets of hessian sacking sewn together, into a special chaff house. It was later used, mixed with chopped turnips to feed to cattle and in its natural state for the deep litter for the chickens. A windy threshing day was a blessing and a curse, depending which job you had, and if you were up, or down, wind. The straw end was usually the down wind side as the tractor radiator had to be kept free and clear of straw bits and chaff to prevent overheating. As a youngster, I always seemed to wind up carrying the chaff. It was light enough, but at the end of the day you had to strip off outside as a ton of chaff would have found its way into every article of clothing you were wearing, including filling the pockets too. Threshing barley was the worst as the barley awns were capable of getting every where, even into your underpants. The sharp spikes would make life very uncomfortable. As I got older I was pressed into all the different jobs except the cutting and feeding of the machine with sheaves. This was the easiest job of all and the cleanest, out of the swirling dust down below and was reserved for the oldest member of the threshing team. All told, a day's threshing was quite an expensive business with a team of about nine or ten men being required.

Before the threshing machines and tractors were affordable to most farmers, threshing contractors were hired. Instead of a tractor, they had a steam engine which used to belch large volumes of coal smoke to add to the threshing dust. The contractors would come, always later than they said they would from some delay at the previous job, and spend up to two weeks with us and thresh the entire harvest. They would bring their own team of workers, usually a bunch of very suspicious looking characters who you couldn't trust at all. Eggs and chickens would start to mysteriously disappear from the farm when they arrived. They were self-contained, living in dilapidated caravans of all descriptions which were set up in a nearby paddock. They had their own cook with them who would stay at the camp, preparing their food, while the rest of us slogged our guts out and filled our lungs with dust. The cook was probably the perpetrator of the missing eggs and chickens but either, we never caught him or never wanted to catch him as, if the threshing team of dubious characters weren't fed on time, they were quite happy to take their pay and walk away.

The team used to spend the entire evening down in the village pub and the locals would find somewhere else to go for the duration of their stay. With a skin full of the best Yorkshire Bitter they soon became raucous and belligerent and many a new morning was greeted with a real shiner of a black eye from the previous evening out. I can well remember the boss man threshing contractor, an absolute giant of a man made bigger by my youthful diminutive size.

He kept law and order in his gang by probably the only way that his men would respect, with a pair of very large, very hard fists. Every so oft, if he felt one of the men was slacking, he would call him round to the back of the stack, the only private place available. The man would return to his job and work like a demon. A lot of the men were returned ex-servicemen who couldn't find jobs elsewhere at that time but had to live somehow. Some of them were very nice, helpful blokes, always ready for a laugh and joke.

These days, the back ache of growing cereals has been taken away. New corn varieties have allowed the farmer to do all the drilling in the autumn when the weather is generally dryer. Huge tractors and chunks of machinery cultivate the soil, fertilize it, spray it for weeds and sow the seed all in one action. In the spring, additional fertilizer is applied with the aid of one ton sacks and a forklift to load up the spreader. Huge combine harvesters, capable of doing thirty acres a day, thresh the grain which is shot into high sided trailers and stored in silos without touching a single grain or piece of straw. The harvester operator sits in his air conditioned, dust free cab with an array of electronic gadgetry to tell him what is happening throughout the machine. I bet half of these

operators couldn't stook a field of sheaves though. But then, that's progress I suppose.

Chapter 7

Potatoes

Potato picking was probably the worst work on the farm. Growing the crop was a relatively simple matter. In accordance with the way crops were rotated through the various fields, the loads of manure from the cattle and pig yards were heaped in large smelly piles in the selected field. The normal place in the rotation was after grass, the humus and the dung from cattle and sheep grazing, adding to the very high fertility required by this crop. Towards the end of autumn, the manure would be spread on the field and then ploughed in, as deep as possible. The ploughing was done so that the turf from the grass was completely buried. By doing this, the maximum amount of soil was available to the keen winter frost and ice. Constant freezing and thawing of the wet soil caused it to expand and contract, leaving a very nice, soft tilth with the minimum of effort. That is really using Mother Nature to do the work for you. These days, the use of high horsepower tractors and rotary tillage tools create the same tilth in a day that took us and Mother Nature all winter. But we didn't burn fossil fuel and pollute the atmosphere.

Fertilizer, in vast quantities, was applied to the field in Spring, as soon as it was dry enough to get onto the land. The fertiliser was harrowed in with a disc harrow and then the field was ridged into high ridges about a yard apart. And they had to be straight too or woe betide the ridger man as all the neighbours would certainly comment if there were kinks in the rows.

"Did tha' get t'lad to do that then?" they would provocatively ask. "Nay, it war t'man, an 'e were thinking abarht thy missus at t'ime" was one of the responses.

"Must 'a bin, 'cos yon 'ump in t'furra looks jus' like 'er backside!" would be the gleeful rejoinder.

The best seed potatoes were always grown in Scotland, high on the hills there and far away from disease. The preferred grade of seed potatoes were small things, the size of a ping-pong ball. If you plant a large potato, you get lots of little potatoes growing. If you plant little seed potatoes you get fewer, but larger potatoes. As the public like fairly large spuds, that's what we tried to grow. The seed potato was placed, by hand, in the bottom of the furrow and then the ridger would be put into the field again to cover the seed by splitting the ridge back. At first, the splitting back was done, not too deep; sufficient to cover the seed with about five inches of soil. As the soil warmed up, the shoots popped their heads out of the soil. When the shoots were out of the ground, so were the weeds. Constant cultivation is required when growing potatoes and, for this reason, the crop is always considered to be a great "land cleaner" as, after this crop, there were very few weeds in the successive crops. The routine was to use a small inter row cultivator which knocked out the weeds, followed up, and straight behind the cultivator, by the ridger again. This process was repeated time after time until the foliage had grown so much that it was no longer possible to get implements into the field without causing damage. The action of constant re-ridging buried the plant with soil and allowed the tubers to form. The more soil, the bigger the crop would be. It was also important to cover the tubers with soil as, a potato exposed to sunlight turns green. There were many nasty stories circulating about green potatoes; the green contained Prussic acid was one, and another, that if a pregnant mother ate them, her child would be deformed. (Spinabifida?)

In these way back days, there was no spray chemical control within easy reach of the average farmer to control weeds. It was done with man power and a swan necked hoe. Disease control was an enormous headache too. The most devastating of all potato diseases is blight. Many will have heard of the Great Famine in Ireland, caused by rampant outbreaks of the blight disease which totally wiped out the national crop of potatoes. Some of the more advanced farmers had a 50 gallon beer cask mounted on the back of a horse drawn cart. Leading from the cask was a pipe, with a tap on it, joined to another pipe held horizontally. This pipe had little holes drilled in it. The cask was filled with a concoction called "Bordeaux Mixture". This was made up on the farm from copper sulphate and freshly burned quicklime. The mixture was made into a "cream" and then diluted with water. The water had to be carried from the farm buildings in cans and the mixture applied under gravity pressure and only went onto the top of the plant. The holes in the distribution pipe clogged up frequently and the application was a long way from being evenly spread and couldn't get underneath the leaves. It was generally considered to be a new fangled silly idea and a complete waste of time and effort. We used copper salts in a powder form to dust the crop. This was done in the early morning when the dew was still on the plants, ensuring that the duster man was wet through inside five minutes, but the dust would stick to the plant. Home-made bags of muslin were tapped with a small stick to produce a fine dust which eventually settled on the plant. It also stuck very well to the operator's now wet clothes and got up his nose too. It was a partially effective way but we still got blight.

The cultivation, dusting, weeding and watching went on all through the summer. In October, the foliage, called "haulm", started to die back, from either natural senescence or disease. Then potato picking would start. The first task was to secure a vast labour force. We would put the word out in the neighbouring villages that we needed pickers and hope to attract most of the available non-working wives. Children were used too, as "Tatie picking" coincided with a ten day school holiday. Several horse and dray teams were sent out every morning to collect the pickers from agreed assembly points in the villages.

Now the picked potatoes were stored in "potato pies" in the farm yard. This was not a culinary delight but a carefully constructed wigwam shaped pile of spuds. The floor was of earth, slightly raised to keep the ground water from running in, sometimes covered with a layer of straw, and a drainage ditch around it too. The sides were covered liberally with loose straw and then the outsides literally thatched with good straight "batts" of straw. If stored potatoes get wet, they rot, very quickly. If they get frosted, they rot even quicker. If inside storage space was available, say inside a barn, this would be used as first choice. It was always necessary to have some of the crop stored in a barn as, in the middle of winter with little else to do on the land, sorting potatoes could be done inside on a wet day.

If it was a rainy morning, and in October and November in Yorkshire, that is not uncommon, a decision had to be made whether to get the labour in or tell it to stay at home. The weather could brighten up within an hour or so and a whole days picking lost. Sometimes the labour made the decision for you as there would be nobody at the collection points on a very wet, miserable morning. The potatoes had to be dry when they were put into the pie or they would rot so there was little point in trying to do any picking if it was really wet.

Prior to the arrival of the labour, the necessary tools were prepared. The tools consisted of the horse drawn potato lifter and baskets. The lifter was a clever machine. A large plough share, digging deep into the row lifted the crop up. Then some metal flails, covered in bits of rubber hose pipe to prevent bruising the crop, would fling the soil and potatoes out to one side. The potatoes would sit on top of the soil ready for picking. The machine only did one row at a time and that row had to be picked before the next row was lifted to prevent the horses from trampling the tubers back into the ground next time around. So the field was split up into sections and several rows were picked at a time, one row from each section. The labour was divided out along the rows and wicker baskets spread out for them. The labour would pick the potatoes into the baskets and leave them where they were when full. Then a horse and cart would travel down the already picked side of the field and each basket tipped into the cart. The baskets, when full, were quite heavy, each weighing about six stones. It took two men to hump them over the cart sides and another man to tip the contents out and throw the basket back onto the ground, away from the approaching horses and lifter. The cart horse would usually drive itself down the row, starting and stopping on voice commands. Bending all day, with only occasional breaks waiting for the lifter or the loading cart, was a back breaking job for the pickers. As the day wore on, you would see people trying to stand upright and holding their aching backs. It was not uncommon to lose half of the picking force on day two as many of them couldn't straighten up when they got out of bed that morning. The more hardy ones stuck it out though. Some of the smarter ones put pads on their knees and crawled through the field all day. That was not a bad idea if the soil was reasonably dry but sticky when a bit damp.

Most of the pickers would bring their own sandwiches with them in the morning along with a glass bottle of hot tea, well wrapped in newspaper and cloths. Tea time was taken sitting on upturned baskets and a great deal of gossiping occurred among the women. Many of them were ex Land Girls looking for a bit of "pin money" as it was called. Interestingly enough, the words "pin money" came into common use many years ago when steel pins were in short supply. The King, can't remember which one, decreed that pins would only be sold on the 1st and 2nd of January each year. The men had to give their wives sufficient money to cover their annual requirements of pins, hence, "pin money".

The girls were a fairly hard bunch too. Potato picking was not for "ladies" at all. Some of the language used would make a sailor blush! Odd shaped potatoes, some resembling certain male or female organs, Would be pocketed until tea time then they would be produced with a variety of crude comments and roars of laughter. The girls also had to go to the loo as well. The loo was usually the nearest, deepest, ditch for a bit of privacy. Any girl heading for the ditch was always ragged unmercifully by the rest of the gang with the few men pickers always offering to help them. If a man headed that way the girls would always rag them too with cries of "Can I hold it for you?" Depending on the popularity and build of the man, the rest of the girls would allude to his manliness by loud comments that it would take two of them or, conversely, they had a pair of tweezers in their handbags! Not for the easily embarrassed or faint hearted. Despite all this badinage, they worked jolly hard and conscientiously tried to collect every available potato. At lunch time the gang would be taken back to the farmyard where some clean dry straw was put into a shed or barn for them. Gallons of tea were prepared in the house and carried in a milk churn to the shed. The pickers would also refill their now empty bottles for the afternoon tea break. Trouble was, the more tea, the more pee, and the less the potatoes that were picked.

The lunch hour was also a danger period as many of the pickers would light cigarettes and, if care was not taken, could cause a barn fire. Some of the girl pickers would take off with the men pickers for secret places unknown during lunch time to do who-knows-what. Of course, everybody guessed and the poor, but satisfied, souls would be ribbed to death for the rest of the afternoon.

My task as a small lad was to tip the baskets out on the cart and then drive the cart to the pie. That was if we had a lot of pickers. If they were short, it was all hands to the picking. I can remember a couple of years when the weather was so wet that picking wasn't completed until just before Christmas and we all got back ache and swore we would never touch another potato until the day we died. That promise was usually broken very quickly at the local Fish and Chip Shop! Who could resist a lovely piece of haddock or hake with plenty of chips, liberally sprinkled with vinegar and salt? And they always tasted better out of a packet wrapped in a piece of newspaper to keep them warm, than out of the modern polystyrene antiseptic containers!

After each field had been picked, a chain harrow was dragged over the field in preparation for sowing winter wheat as quickly as possible. The harrowing did two things; firstly it rolled up the dead haulm so that it could be either carted off the field or burned on the spot. Secondly, it brought to the surface any potatoes that had been missed at picking and so these had to be collected too. In a wet year, potatoes were worth their weight in gold as the chances were that the national crop would have been badly blighted and therefore in short supply. In such bad times, the potato merchant would be breathing down your neck for supplies and would position his truck at the entrance to the field and take the crop, soil and all, straight off the land. That was always a labour saver but it didn't always pay to do it from an economic standpoint unless his price was very good.

With the harvest safely home, neatly tucked up into their pies against the ravages of the weather, the crop was now ready for sorting and selling. The pies, built in the stack yards, were only opened up on dry, frost free days. The old potato sorter would be dragged into place. This was a rather cumbersome looking piece of machinery, consisting of a long rotating tube of wire mesh set at an incline. The mesh was of ever increasing size so that, as the potatoes and soil were shovelled in at the top end, the soil fell onto the floor first. Then the smallest potatoes would be riddled out and bagged off. Then the next size up and so on, until the first grade and largest potatoes came out of the back end of the machine. These went up a small canvas elevator where any bad ones, and there were always plenty of those, and stones, were picked off before the good crop was caught into sacks. As the day wore on, the machine had to be cleaned out, all the soil removed, and the whole contraption moved further down to the face of the pie.

It was slow tedious work. Rotten potatoes have a terrible smell too. There would always be some part of the pie where the rain had leaked through or where the frost had been able to penetrate. The potatoes here went very soft, a runny, slimy sort of softness with the stench to match. We all wore aprons, made out of an old piece of hessian sack, tied around the waist with a bit of twine. At least it was something to wipe your hands on throughout the day but you soon became a walking odour carrier. It was the shoveller-in mans job to prevent these badly rotted spuds from entering the machine as, if they went in, the machine would soon clog up. Then everything, big ones, middle ones and small ones, plus clods of soil, would find their way onto the picking elevator and into the sack. The machine was driven by muscle power, a huge wheel drove the riddle and the elevator. This was driven by chains from a smaller crank with a wooden handle set into it. It was heavy work and the men would rotate jobs every fifteen minutes or so. In later years we were all delighted when a small chug-chug diesel engine was purchased to do the hard work. Working outside, we could warm our hands on the exhaust pipe. Working inside, the damned diesel engine nearly gassed us all and made us partially deaf after a long day sorting spuds. Still, anything was better than cranking that handle!

The Ministry of Agriculture came up with a price support scheme, to try to even out the seasonal marketing peaks and troughs. In years of huge surpluses, you could apply to the Ministry for a subsidy on the ware, or saleable, potatoes that there was no market for. This was the biggest money spinner out. The idea was that you sorted your potatoes to market quality standards and then applied to the Ministry to feed them to your own cattle. The spuds were riddled out, sometimes not too carefully, and many of the undersized ones found their way into the bag as well. The bags were left untied, standing up in rows. The "Man from the Ministry" would come and would inspect several bags to make sure that the sorting job had been done properly. Of course, if you stacked the bags close together in the barn, made sure there was little or no light in the place and made access to the bags at the rear of the barn an obstacle course to get to, then he would only inspect the ones he could get at. So, you made certain that the bags at the front were a very good sample. When satisfied, he would then have to make sure that the potatoes were dyed with a purple dye by tipping some of the made up liquid from a watering can into each bag

Now the dye was quite potent stuff and the Ministry Man, in his hacking jacket, cord trousers and nice clean shoes, certainly didn't want that on his clothes, so, you offered to do it for him. By now, he was probably making out the paper work which had to be done and so, when he wasn't watching, you would deliberately miss out splashing the dye on as many bags as you could! When he had left, these undyed bags were dragged aside and not used for cattle food at all but sold to the local Chip Shop for cash in the dark of the night. Sometimes they were presented for dying next time round. Which ever way, the Ministry must have lost millions of Pounds as every farmer I knew was doing the same thing! The national yield and production statistics must have been a total load of manure too. Many farmers justified their actions by saying that the government took too much from them in taxes anyway so it was only getting back a bit of what you had paid out. Remembering that most farmers were church going, God fearing people, it brought a new meaning to the word "hypocrisy".

So what happens today? Pre-sprouted seed potatoes are planted by machine, that gets them growing faster and earlier in the season. Disease and weed control is a simple, if expensive matter, with high pressure sprayers directing chemicals to the exact spot where it is needed. Potatoes are picked using machines with X-ray beams being able to decide, as quick as a flash, what is a spud and what is a stone. The crop is washed, and dried by automated machines and stored in heated and ventilated sheds, all in boxes handled with forklifts. The sorting is done into little paper sacks tied with wire at the top. The fast food chains demand varieties of potatoes that don't absorb much fat. The housewife wants pre cooked, deep frozen ready chopped oven baking chips. The old Fish and Chip shop has gone and the law prevents you from using newspaper to wrap them in anyway!

"Three pennyworth o' chips an' a nice piece of cod, please"

Chapter 8

Hay

Haymaking has certainly got to be one of the most pleasant, but most frustrating tasks in farming. Pleasant, for who, except the most allergic, hay fever riddled people in the world, can fail to relish the smell of newly mown grass. Frustrating, as the quality of the made hay is totally dependant on the whims and fancies of the weather.

Hay in Yorkshire was a late June to early July job. On infrequent occasions, an early spring and good grass growth would push the farming clock forward and Mother Nature's clock was not to be tampered with like a mechanical one. When it was ready to go, it was time to go. Before the modern varieties of grasses were spawned, a good grass pasture consisted of a mixture of grass varieties; Italian Rye Grass, Cocksfoot, Timothy, Meadow Fescue, Smooth Broome and, of course, the clovers, red and white. Each grass was grown for its individual flavour or palatability, the protein content and its leafiness and bulking ability. A good, mixed, perennial pasture would last for years if well maintained. To an outsider, grass is green stuff that cows eat and has to be easy to grow because I've got it growing in my garden! But nutritious grass requires a lot of planning and hard work. Good land preparation to ensure the field is smooth and level enough to run a mower over it was essential. No good having a good crop that you couldn't cut. Sowing grass seed onto a field was a very tricky job indeed.

The seeds themselves are tiny little things, like pinheads. And grass seed was very expensive too. After a great deal of deliberation and talking to the

seed merchant, a mixture, for a specific pasture, would be carefully weighed out and mixed into small linen bags. Then a lot of bargaining for the best price always took place. There was never anything such as a list price, everything was negotiable. I learned that you always asked for discount on every single thing ever bought. It's remarkable how often you can get it too. Years later, I embarrassed my wife no end by asking for discount on a pair of socks in a large store. She was equally embarrassed when I was given it!

The seed had to be sown on to the field on a windless day. We used a thing called a "fiddle drill" to do this. This contraption was light enough for a man to sling around his neck on the straps provided for the purpose. It consisted of a bag, to hold the seed, and a disc, which would spin around and scatter the seed as it was allowed to fall onto it from the bag. The disc was driven by a bow, exactly like the bow of a violin or cello, drawn back and forth, the string of the bow wrapped around the shaft of the disc causing it to spin. Hence the name " Fiddle Drill". A very simple and efficient gadget. The skill in the application was pre-preparation. Firstly, the field was marked out with sticks at each end so that a straight walking line could be maintained. Then, the steps and the fiddling had to be calculated by trial and error so that the correct rate of application was achieved. Not an easy task at all. At the end of sowing a fifteen acre paddock, the man doing it must have walked miles. Have you ever tried to walk in a straight line watching a fixed object in front of you? Sounds very easy but try it some day. It was easier to do, like long army route marches, if you hummed a little song to yourself in time to the walking and fiddling.

Applying the seed evenly was very important to give the pasture a good start to life. Once it was well established, maintaining even growth was equally difficult to achieve as, when animals graze it, their droppings fertilize only a small area. And it needs a lot of feeding and liming to keep out all the unwanted weeds. The worst weeds in grasslands must be thistles, nettles and dock plants. All of the above will proliferate without the timely application of lime to ensure that the soil is not overly acidic. Grass needs nitrogenous fertilizers in large quantities too as it is the nitrogen, albeit working in conjunction with all the other chemical elements, that has the most effect in producing a lot of green matter. So, we regularly ran a chain harrow over such grazed pastures to spread the naturally dropped manure and pull out all the dead grass before fertilizing it again. Lime was applied before sowing the grass seed to correct the acidity and a good dollop of fertilizer applied as soon as spring showed any sign of arriving to get it growing.

The weather at haymaking time is something that only romantics and poets enthuse about. If you are lucky to get a few weeks of good weather, then it is worth romanticising over. Otherwise, you want to cry as you watch a field of good grass getting darker and darker in colour as all the nutritious bits are washed out and it starts to rot. The trick to high protein hay was to cut it just as the seeds were fully formed and certainly before they matured. That was the theory. In practise, if the crop was anywhere near ready and the weather men said we were in for a prolonged fine spell, the mower was out in a flash. Drop everything, make hay while the sun shines. Never a truer adage. In good weather, excellent hay can be made in less than a week. Within half a day of it being cut it, was fluffed up with a machine called a "tedder". In good drying weather, hot, and a nice wind blowing, the hay could be tedded twice or three times a day to keep turning the damp green bits on the bottom to the top to let the sun have a go at it and to let the wind blow through it. As soon as it was dry, and I mean really dry, it was banged onto carts and put into the barns, even if it meant working until eleven o'clock at night to do it. In a wet year, to keep the hay off the ground and to try to get what little wind and sun there was onto it, we had to "cock" the hay. Cocking was done using a tripod of longish sticks cut from the wood for the purpose. The hay was raked into heaps and then stacked onto the tripod with a hay fork. It was a very slow and labour consuming task.

My jobs as a "little 'un" were dogsbody jobs. Take a rake and rake the hay out of the corners of the field and from under the hedgerow. I had to take the tea out to the fields too, usually on the back of a horse. Without the luxury of a riding saddle, my little legs would be stretched horizontally across its broad back. I was thrown on, given a basket containing the tea and food and warned not to drop it under any circumstances. This was a very important job, or so I felt, as the welcome I always got from the men in the fields made me feel as if I was their daily saviour! I always prided myself that the tea was still too hot to drink by the time I got it to them. To avoid dropping it meant walking the horse slowly. How many small boys can possibly resist the urge to make the horse "go" a bit? Sure enough, I got the horse into a trot and sure enough I fell off the horse. Now maybe that's not strictly true. As we were trotting along, being bounced up and down, the basket, carried in front of me, started to slip off the horses back. Trying to slow the horse down by hauling back on the reins wasn't very effective as she was a strong mouthed old nag at the best of times. The basket was heavy and slipped down the side of the horse. To save everything from being smashed to bits, (remember, these are pre-plastic days), I did the honourable thing and bailed out, somehow managing to hang onto the basket.

Now the field was a long way away and, being unable to re-mount the horse, was faced with having to carry the basket in one hand and hang on to the reins as I led the horse too. If the tea was cold on arrival, I knew I would get some stick, verbally and maybe physically too from the men in the field. So, I trudged on for what seemed to be miles and miles and miles. The basket got heavier and heavier and to change carrying hands meant I had to stop the horse, walk round to the other side of it, swap hands, walk on again. My arms got more and more tired as we made slow progress, I really thought there was no way I would ever get to the field when suddenly, we were there. What a relief it was to have overcome the falling off and having made the objective with still fairly hot tea. I put the basket down under the shade of a big tree and went to tie the horse to the hedge. The men were approaching, looking forward to a welcome break when the horse stepped backwards and put it's hoof right into the basket and smashed the lot. I cried. I was allowed to at four years old but didn't get any sympathy at all. Unceremoniously, I was thrown onto the horse, given the basket, the horse's backside was slapped to make it really go, and sent back to fetch some more. "And be sharp about it, too" were the last words I heard as I left the field hanging onto the horse's mane for dear life.

I think my pride was really hurt from this incident. Many years later, I learned a word, "hubris". My dictionary today tells me it means "insolent pride or security, arrogance". What it really means is that when you are on top, be careful because, if you fall off your little pedestal, it's very hard work getting back up again! I suppose that is the sort of learning curve we all go through one way or another. How often does it occur in life?

The hay, when dry and ready, would be loaded onto carts by hand using hay forks. The man stacking it would carefully place it around the edges of the cart first and then fill up the centre as the sides grew. When the load was too high for the men with the forks to reach the top, the sides of the load were cleaned of any loose and falling bits and then it was away to the farm yard and the barns. Sometimes the hay would have to be stacked in the yard if all the barns were full but this was avoided wherever possible as hay soon deteriorates if left out in the open, no matter how well you thatched the stack. We always tried to get the hay home too. Many farmers made a stack in the field. While it saved time during haymaking, it was a damned nuisance having to trek to the field in the depths of winter to fetch hay. Also, the local courting population thought that such hay stacks had been built simply for their convenience and pleasure, and a carelessly thrown match or cigarette end would soon make short work out of a good stack of hay.

Many an old farmer would have given his arm for some of the haymaking machinery of today. The grass is no sooner cut than a conditioning machine is put through it which squeezes and crimps the grass, allowing the sap and moisture to dry out quickly. It's fluffed up and windrowed into rows as light as a feather duster with fast high powered machines. Huge round bales are used and to keep the weather off the finished material, and you can even get a machine which will put the big round bale into a plastic bag for you.

No more lying on your back on top of a cart load of hay as it sways its way slowly down the track. No time to look up at the clouds and make pictures and shapes out of them and dream. No more clandestine kisses and cuddles under a haystack either.

Chapter 9
Pigs

Of all the animals on a farm the pig is probably the most maligned of them all. When wishing to compare a human being's bad manners to that of an animal, we immediately liken them to the poor old pig. Let's dispel a few of these wicked mis-truths right from the start.

Pigs are the cleanest of all the farm animals. They are the only farm animal who has a well defined toilet area in their pens. They will select one corner, and, either indoor or outdoors, that is the area which is used. Their sleeping area is kept extraordinarily clean and dry and is usually as far away from the toilet area as they can get it. They have a play area too, in between the sleeping and toilet zones. Just like a good house lay-out. What gives pigs their bad reputations is the way we human beings treat them! I will concede that their eating habits tend to be a little noisy and somewhat indelicate though. That is due to the shape of their mouths and the kind of food they are given to eat. They have to use their bottom jaws to scoop up the meal and water mixture which they are frequently fed on. Try eating sloppy porridge from a dish without a spoon and without using your hands and see what sort of a mess you will make too! Because their troughs are set on the ground, as the pig takes a mouthful, it has to lift up its head to swallow. A sloppy meal-and-water mix is bound to spill out of their mouths as they lift their heads. Have you ever tried eating something from the floor, on your knees, with your hands behind your back? I will wager that you will lift your head to get it down your gullet too.

The natural cleanliness of a pig can be used to the farmer's advantage to save him considerable time and labour. Some have a row of piggeries and each pen consists of a warm sleeping area under cover. In the little back yard is their feeding trough and water point and the slope of the floor is such that any water drains down to the end of the yard. The side fences of each yard can be constructed out of metal gates and the pen gate, when closed, restricts the pigs to their sleeping area. To clean out several hundred pigs is a relatively simple affair. Starting at one end, walk down closing all the gates so that you now have a long passageway of concrete with all the pig manure right there. It is then a simple matter to take a tractor mounted scraper and by running straight down this passage, clean out the pens in one pass. Depending on the design of the buildings, the manure can be pushed straight into a trailer or a muck spreader, positioned at the end of the passage and Hi Ho! off to the field you go!

These days a lot of the farms use water as a medium to shift this manure too and this is put straight into slurry tanks and spread that way. And does it ever smell! No such thing as sweet countryside fragrances if you are down wind of a pig farm using the slurry system.

Going back many years though, it wasn't as easy as that. As a lad, I can well remember that we had all our pigs in small pens or boxes which were constructed around the perimeter of a large, closed-in yard, called a fold yard. These boxes had to be cleaned out by hand on a daily basis. This was done with a fork, shovel and brush and the manure thrown into a wheelbarrow and carted to a muck heap or midden. Having to carry three hand tools was a bit of a poser as, if you left them for a couple of minutes unattended, the pigs, out of curiosity would nudge them around until they fell into the manure. The tools then had to be cleaned off before further use. Anyway, only sissies wore gloves and the manure was "just good clean pig s..t" I was regularly told. At the end of a "mucking out" session I was not allowed into the house until I had stripped off the entire outer layer of clothing, and she didn't care what the weather was like out there. Thank goodness in later life for nylon overalls, gumboots, automatic washing machines and tumble driers! A set of overalls could, and would, be washed and dried over the lunch hour if necessary.

Each pig pen had a wooden half door, secured by two bolts, one top, one bottom. The bottom of the door was lined with galvanised metal as the pigs' favourite pastime was cutting their teeth on the door and they could chew it to bits in no time at all. The door had to fit into a small step slightly lower than the pen itself and the cross bracing and supports were always on the outside. The reason for this was the pig's nose. Of all animals the pig has the strongest of noses. They soon learn to put their noses under a door or under the braces and use their considerable neck strength to lift the door right off its hinges. The tops of the doors had to be high enough and strong enough to withstand the weight of a pig too. Being very inquisitive and gregarious animals, a pig, if allowed to, will stand on its hind legs and place its front feet on top of the door and see what is going on in the outside world. One very simple rule when building anything for pigs was, build it strong and secure everything down.

We had a sixty sow herd. That was enough too as they easily filled every nook and cranny we had with their progeny. The "dry" sows, those who were pregnant and awaiting their next litter, were all kept in two large yards divided by a gate. The freshly weaned sows were in one half and those in a more advanced state of pregnancy were in the other part. This was done to be able to give those who were close to having a litter, a better diet. You couldn't give them all the same diet and if you did, they would soon become unhealthily fat and your bank balance unhealthily thin.

As the sows came close to farrowing, a term used for having the litter, we would move the sow into a special building which was equipped with farrowing crates. Mother pigs can be huge animals in comparison to their off-spring. As she has to lie down to allow the piglets to feed, it was a very real danger that she could, and often did, lie on her litter and kill several of them. A bad trait of some pigs, as well, is to eat the youngsters as they are born! Such sows were very quickly sent to market.

A farrowing crate is a metal frame with bars at the bottom to allow the piglets to get out from underneath mother, large enough to allow the sow to lie down but not big enough for her to turn around in. Next to the crate was a small area which was kept as draught proof as possible using slot together wooden planks, and above this, we put some batts of straw as a low ceiling. New born piglets are very susceptible to the cold, especially in the winters of Yorkshire. The piglets soon learn that the warmest place to sleep is in this secluded nursery area, called a creep. If the ceiling was made too high, the heat would be dissipated. This was easy to spot as the piglets would lie in a heap to get body heat from the ones on top. This was always amusing to see as they would be stacked three high, the biggest always at the bottom and the poor little runt at the top of the heap getting colder. If they got up for a session at mother's milk bar the big ones would re-enter the heap of piglets by pushing their noses into the bottom and worming their way in. If they were at the right temperature, they would be somewhat spread out but still comfortably touching each other in a friendly, family togetherness fashion.

There has to be a lesson in life for us here. If you are born big and strong the chances are that you are going to get bigger and stronger. If you are the runt of the family, you are not going to get your fair share of life right from the very start unless you are very determined about living.

This sensitivity to the temperature is not confined only to newly born pigs. Even the older ones do not grow and perform very well at low temperatures. Ideally, we used to try for an air temperature of about sixty five degrees Fahrenheit for the newly born piglets which would give them about eighty degrees Fahrenheit in a straw nest. To achieve this, the floors of the farrowing pens were always insulated. Before polystyrene foam was invented, we used to insert straw between two layers of concrete and what a difference it used to make too. It was the same principle as a mattress on a bed; the more coverings below you, the warmer you are.

We always kept sows with twelve or fourteen teats as we felt this was enough and not too many. The back two teats were often dry anyway. If the sow had a litter of, say, ten piglets, then theoretically there are enough teats to go round and a couple of spares. If the supply to one teat was dry then the biggest piglets would always push a smaller one away and latch onto its food supply. Again, the poor little runt would always be pushed out. It was a wonder they ever survived at all. Sometimes they didn't. If they were too runty, we would end their days prematurely, there and then, as, in later life, they would become the object of bullying for the rest of the litter and may have pieces bitten off them. Also, when you are short of room, a runt is taking up space which should be occupied by a better meat producer.

As pigs are very family orientated animals, mixing two or more litters after weaning always caused a riot. The two litters would fight until individual animals had established their hierarchal positions. No such thing as democracy for them. The bigger and more aggressive you were, the higher up the pecking order you went. Once this hierarchy had been established, a lesser pig would give way to a superior pig at the trough without too much bother. A wise farmer always ensured that the trough space was adequate to accommodate all the litters to prevent such in-fighting. As we would often simultaneously mix three or four litters together for fattening purposes, it would take the piglets at least a day, if not two, to sort themselves out. The biggest and strongest always got the most food and so grew bigger and stronger. They got their come-uppance in the end as they were the first to be sent off to market! But they were the most productive and healthiest pigs of the lot.

About three weeks after they were born the pigs were given an injection of iron. Most pigs kept indoors seem to suffer from an iron deficiency and a sow's milk contains virtually no iron. The old fashioned way was to cut a grass sod from a paddock or just a shovelful of soil each day and feed that to the sow and the little ones. Then chemistry took over and the injection was certainly more effective if a little more expensive. The little devils used to scream their heads off as soon as you touched them and it was on such occasions that you were thankful for the farrowing crate as mother would get quite agitated and would just as soon bite your leg off as look at you. If this screaming was bad the next was even worse.

We had to castrate the male pigs as they become sexy little beasts at a very early age and the butchers said that boar meat was too strong in taste. This was a two man Saturday morning job. One man would sit on a straw bale with the piglet, head down, clamped between his legs. He would hold on to the back legs, one in each hand and try to stop the piglet from moving. The "knife" man, armed with one of those old fashioned razor blades which had only one cutting edge and a roll of metal where the other edge should have been, would sit facing the holding man. The piglet's scrotum was cut, as small a cut as possible, directly over one testicle. The first testicle was squeezed out and the cord severed with a scraping action. Then a second cut was made inside the little scrotum to pop out the second testicle which was dealt with in the same fashion. The cut was liberally sloshed with a strong disinfectant and the piglet released to go hopping and wriggling about for a couple of hours. This didn't hurt at all, unless the piglet squirmed too much and the "knife" man cut himself.

Like the story of the camel herder in the desert who was asked by a tourist how he castrated his camels.

"You stand behind the animal with two rocks, one in each hand and clap them together", said the herder.

"That must hurt" said the enquirer with a pained look on his face. "Oh, no", said the herder. "Not unless you get your thumb in the way"!

In the spring and through to the early autumn, we often let the dry sows live outside in a paddock. You had to pick a paddock that was going to be ploughed up that autumn as the sows would make a terrible mess of the field. Their noses are ideal digging tools and they would dig up the paddock in their quest for juicy, tender roots and shoots. They slept in things called "Pigloos", several sheets of curved corrugated iron bolted together with only one end section. There was enough room for two sows in each Pigloo and, like teenage girls in boarding school dormitories; they picked their sleeping mates very carefully. A pair of sows would stick together in the same dormitory for as long as they could, or like girls, until they fell out over who knows what kind of porcine disagreement. Maybe one had accused the other of snoring or something. Shade trees for summer were a prime requisite in the paddock. Pigs suffer from sunstroke! To protect themselves they would find or make a mud hole and when hot and sunny, coat themselves with Mother Nature's finest suntan cream. And then what a sight they looked. Remember that mud is not dirt or dirty. It is a natural solution to a natural problem to a pig.

Pigs are almost impossible animals to try to drive or lead from one place to another. They have a brain though, and can see that if the way in front or to the side is blocked by something solid, then they don't go that way. So, the method of moving a pig is with pig boards. These are pieces of plywood with a handle sawn into them or anything else light enough to carry such as a piece of corrugated iron sheet. With two boards, and keeping as close to the pig as possible, you could keep her nose pointing towards the only unblocked way, forward. To make her turn a corner, put the board in front of her. Easy! Until, of course, she becomes totally obstinate and resists passively by refusing to budge. It's hard work pushing a two hundred and fifty pound sow from the summer paddock to the buildings when she wants to stay in the holiday camp. Or, alternatively, she would take off like a rocket down the track with you trailing behind with your tin sheet hindering any speedy progress.

Pigs love to play games. I suppose if we were confined to a pen for days on end we would also invent some game to play to relieve the boredom. The first sort of play is the scrapping and fighting which little boys and puppy dogs indulge in. The trouble with this form of play is that as soon as one pig loses its sense of humour, it turns into a knock-down, drag-out, no-holds-barred, honest to goodness barney. This frequently resulted in torn ears and chewed tails and, of course, the loss of weight gain from the tension and stress. Once a pig had its tail bitten it seemed as though all the other pigs were intent on deepening the wound and sometimes the pig finished up with only a stump of a tail. If the pigs were in a yard, deep with straw, they would suddenly take it upon themselves, for no apparent rhyme or reason to go galloping about the yard screaming and grunting like banshees. Then, suddenly, they would all stop, absolutely still, and then take off again. Straw and dust would fly everywhere and the pigs would look at you with a smile on their faces.

To help prevent boredom, we gave them toys, just like indulgent parents. We would hang old car tyres on chains from the beams above. This was used as a pig "punch bag" as they would charge it, bite it, butt it and generally do everything they could to it including trying to pull it down. It did have the desired effect though of giving them some object to play with other than each others' ears and tails! In the fields we would put a few decent sized round logs of wood. The sows loved to stick their noses under them and roll them to see what was underneath. Then they would use them as scratching posts for their heads. The shade trees were always in considerable danger of losing bark too as the pigs found them ideal back and side scratchers. When we put them into the apple orchard to clean up the windfalls, we had to protect the apple trees with barbed wire otherwise they would chew away at the trunk until they ring-barked the tree which would then die. Before we had pigs, we had daffodils in the apple orchard which used to give us a great deal of pleasure in the spring. The pigs soon found the bulbs and that was the end of that. Whose idea was it to put the pigs in the orchard anyway?

On cold nights, and there were plenty of those in Yorkshire, we would throw extra straw bales into the pig yards for bedding. We didn't have to spread the straw as the pigs soon made a splendid job of that rooting into it to find whatever tasty morsels live in straw bales. Then they would bury themselves into the straw so that you couldn't see them at all. First thing in the morning, if you were early and quiet that is, it would give you a bit of a start as there wasn't a pig to be seen. Thoughts of "pignapping" and rustlers flashed through your head. The first sound of a clanging feed bucket would be followed by a total volcanic eruption of the straw in the yard as dozens of pigs emerged from their night beds. Then the noise started.

You could set your watch by the pigs' appetites. They knew when it was feeding time as they quickly got used to a routine. If you were late they would tell you, loudly and ear splittingly so. This made Sunday morning feeding into a real chore. It was bad enough to have to put up with any noise with a hangover from the Saturday night festivities. We always had an extra hour in bed on a Sunday morning, a very civilised thing to do. The pigs however were not working on the standard calendar or clock and couldn't give a damn if it was Tuesday or

Sunday. They were hungry and just wanted their food. If you were late, and had to walk into one of the yards with food, you could get mobbed and the food could be tipped out as several pigs tried to get their heads into the buckets as you were carrying them to the troughs. Some of them would also get a bit carried away and have a little nip at your legs too, as if you were the hors d'oeuvre.

Pigs can bite, very badly. We had one incident which was not funny at all. One of our lasses was feeding some sows and we had the boar pig in the yard with them at the time. As she walked in front of the beast, the boar took a big piece of flesh, as big as the palm of your hand, from her thigh. This bled profusely and caused a great deal of concern as we rushed her off to hospital. She was stitched up and after a few tetanus jabs was taken home for a week. When she came back to work she was, understandably, very nervous about going into any pen with the boar pig in it. One of the old hands sat her down and talked to her at length about what action to take to overcome this phobia. Basically, the gist of his advice was that she had to show the boar who was the boss. In order to do this, he armed her with the wooden fencing hammer we used for knocking in fencing stakes. This was not exactly a light toy but she wasn't exactly a dainty lady either.

She went into the pen and walked straight up to the boar. The boar glared at her as if remembering that this lass had a nice soft tender thigh. Then she hit the boar as hard as she could on the head with the hammer shouting at it as loudly as she could. The boar staggered and shook its head but didn't move. She raised the hammer again and gave it another good crack. The boar started to back off. As she raised the hammer again, still shouting at it, the boar decided that he had met his match and backed off altogether. After this "hammering", when the lass walked into the pen, all she had to do was to shout at the boar and he would back off, well away from her. Cruel justice perhaps but how else could she have mastered this huge animal?

A boar pig is a very big and strong animal weighing in at over five hundred pounds and their job was to serve the sows. This seemed to bring out primeval instincts in them. They were naturally fighting to protect, and show, their superiority as they would in the wild. Boar pigs have very well developed incisor teeth, presumably remnants of the tusks of their forefathers. After this incident we called the vet who, with the aid of a knock out injection and a four pound hammer, removed the fang-like teeth. Subsequently, we would never buy or rear a boar unless its teeth had been snipped off at birth. In fact, many pig breeders would snip the incisor teeth off all their newly born pigs and their breeding sows too, just for safety.

Despite this occasional display of viciousness and bad temper, pigs can make excellent house pets, if the fancy takes you that is. It never appealed to me and the "Boss" would have had my guts for garters if this had ever been suggested. I did know a bachelor farm chap who had one though. He called it Porky, well, what else would you call a pet pig? I don't know the true story about how he got the pig in the first place. He always said he won it in a raffle and didn't quite know what to do with it. This pet pig grew up with his dogs and thought it was one too. It would sleep in the kitchen with the dogs, would ask to be let out to do its business and scratched at the door to be let back in again. Otherwise, it roamed his small house as would a lap dog. It would sleep on the carpet in front of the fire, quite contentedly until it heard something outside. Whether it got this from the dogs or not, if there was somebody outside it would grunt away at the door until it was satisfied.

He had the pig ringed, that is, "a ring at the end of his nose, his nose, a ring at the end of his nose." This stopped the pig from rooting up the small garden. The pig would sit watching the fellow eat his food and wait for the occasional scrap from the table which it had learned to catch as it was thrown, just like a dog. If it didn't catch the morsel, it knew that one of the dogs would beat it to getting the morsel off the floor. I had the experience of sharing the man's evening meal once and could hardly eat for watching this show going on. When the pig was small it used to chase its own tail, round and round it went and never had a hope of success but it was a good party trick. As Porky became a bit older and bigger, he did become a bit of a problem, space wise, in the house. It was like somebody owning a St. Bernard dog in a two up, two down cottage.

I had asked him what he was going to do with the pig, long term. When he got it, the story was that as soon as it was old enough to fend for itself, he would put it in with other similar aged pigs on the farm. This never happened as he became very attached to his pet to the extent that he didn't go away on holiday that year, as nobody volunteered to house sit his pet in their home. What kind of friends did he have? The pig grew bigger and bigger until it was nearly at bacon size, now about one hundred and fifty pounds and nearly six months old. Porky had to go, but who was going to do it and how? The man couldn't bring himself to take it to market so we did it for him. He made quite sure that he wasn't there the day we arrived with the trailer to take Porky away. He had said that he didn't want the money that the pig would fetch at the market but we felt we couldn't keep it either. So we deliberately fiddled his overtime for a few months until the cash had been paid out. He never made any mention at all of Porky for many years. When he retired, he went to live with his sister in a village several miles away and we knew we wouldn't see him again as it was a long way to cycle and there was no public transport either. As he was saying his goodbyes to us, almost as an aside, he asked if we remembered his Porky. How could we forget!

He said, "I allus meant t'ask yer 'ow much 'e fetched at t'market". When we told him and explained how we had paid him for the pig, he was totally unconcerned about the money. With a faraway look in his eyes, a little moist perhaps, but then he did have conjunctivitis, he just said, "Aye, 'e were a right good pal that pig were" and left it at that. Since then, I've heard of other people keeping pigs as pets but only on TV shows.

Pigs have an interesting history. The wild pig was a forest animal feeding on acorns, roots, worms and even small mammals if they didn't get out of the way fast enough. The pig, unlike a cow or a sheep, is a non ruminant and its digestive system is very similar to that of a human being. The present day commercial pig bears little resemblance to its antecedents who hailed mainly from Europe, North Africa and South East Asia. Humans have kept pigs for their own use since Neolithic times, way back in the late Stone Age, and bones have been found which, when reconstructed, showed a very different pig. It had long legs, a long snout, heavy shoulders but very light hind quarters and was covered in bristles. In later years, in the Middle Ages, pigs were herded in the vast forests of oak and beech trees by the swineherd. About two hundred years ago, travellers brought back, from their sea voyages, animals from the Far East, mainly China. These pigs were much smaller than the pigs kept in England at that time but had a tendency to mature quicker although they did put on a lot of fat too. The cross breeding of the old English pig and these new imports gave rise to a smaller but more meaty and slightly fattier animal than had been kept to that date. In more recent times, around fifty to a hundred years ago, the Scandinavians, especially the Swedish and Danish farmers, bred a pig known as the Swedish Landrace. A far longer bodied pig, excellent for bacon. It has now been bred on so that it is an ideal dual purpose animal for both pork and bacon.

A porker is usually a shorter bodied pig such as the Berkshire and Middle White breeds. Bacon pigs came from the Large Whites, Tamworth, Welsh and Landrace types, all of which are very much longer in the body and so produced more bacon from the ribs and belly. If a pork breed is kept too long it becomes very fatty, which is not needed. In contrast, if a bacon pig is not kept long enough, it is all bone and no meat. So the farmer had to decide which type of market he was aiming for and select his breed accordingly. Also, was he going to keep his pigs indoors or out doors? As mentioned previously, white pigs can suffer from the effects of the sun, getting sun stroke rather badly, and are therefore more suited to being indoors all the time. Pigs do come in other colours too. The Berkshire and the Large Black are both black or a reddish black colour. The Tamworth, a native of the Birmingham area, is a chestnut red and a very pretty pig if you like that sort of thing. Then there are those who don't know what to be, the Essex and the Wessex both having "saddlebacks" of either black backs and white feet or white backs with black feet. The trouble with the darker pigs is that the pigmentation can, and does quite often, carry through into the meat and may discolour it, especially around the belly area. But they have the advantage of avoiding the sun stroke problems.

The market for pig meat has changed throughout the ages too. In pre- war days, the North of England wanted, and got, a large fatty pig for bacon. The South of England preferred a longer, leaner pig for the Wiltshire ham trade. Then there was the "cutter", rather like a Wiltshire ham pig but used mainly for fresh meat as its size and weight were very indeterminate. Finally there was the London "porker", a smaller pig of about one hundred pounds which was kept solely for the fresh pork meat market. These days, the pig breeds are a lot more flexible and in keeping with modern fads and worries about cholesterol and diets, are much less fatty. A mature pig can weigh in at six to seven hundred pounds, especially boars which have been known to top the half ton mark! That's an awful lot of pig. Today, a pig of one hundred and twenty five pounds is well received by the market for a good pork roast.

There is an old saying that the only part of a pig that is not used is its squeak. Everything else is edible or has some alternative function. Other than the usual cuts for chops, roasts, bacon, and hams, the rest of the pig can be made into sausages and brawn and the fat into lard. Some people consider pig's trotters and "chapps", the head and jaws, to be a delicacy and, of course, pork spare ribs done with a piquant sauce over a barbecue are decidedly mouth watering. The skin can be cured into some of the finest leather, much desired for gloves and luggage. The bristles are much sought after as they make very fine paint brushes. The Chinese and Japanese forms of brush writing give a ready market there too. So all that remains is the squeak and that usually stays as a reminder to the farmer to feed his pigs on time!

Pigs are very sensitive creatures and suffer very badly from stress. If you try to mix several pens of pigs just before going to market you can be assured that some will have died of stress before they get off the truck. Firstly, they fight and secondly the stress of loading them, getting them to a noisy market on a noisy truck travelling in noisy traffic is just too much for their nerves. And you can't blame them. Modern life is stressful enough for us, it's a nightmare for a pig. Way back when, we used to quietly load the pen of pigs, all of whom had been together for a long time, and then gently drive them to the market. Instead of driving the pigs into a sale ring, the buyers and auctioneers would go to the pigs, moving from pen to pen, selling them as they walked down the rows. Today, it seems that most of the pigs are produced and sent to a special abattoir on a contractual basis, which is far less stressful for the pig. If their adrenalin is still chasing around their bodies, the meat doesn't taste half as good and, I am told, goes bad very quickly too.

There was one producer of pig meat who used to advertise that his pork products came "From Pigs That Died Happy".

As a boy I couldn't understand how anything could be happy to die. Now I can see that it was a very clever and knowledgeable advertisement.

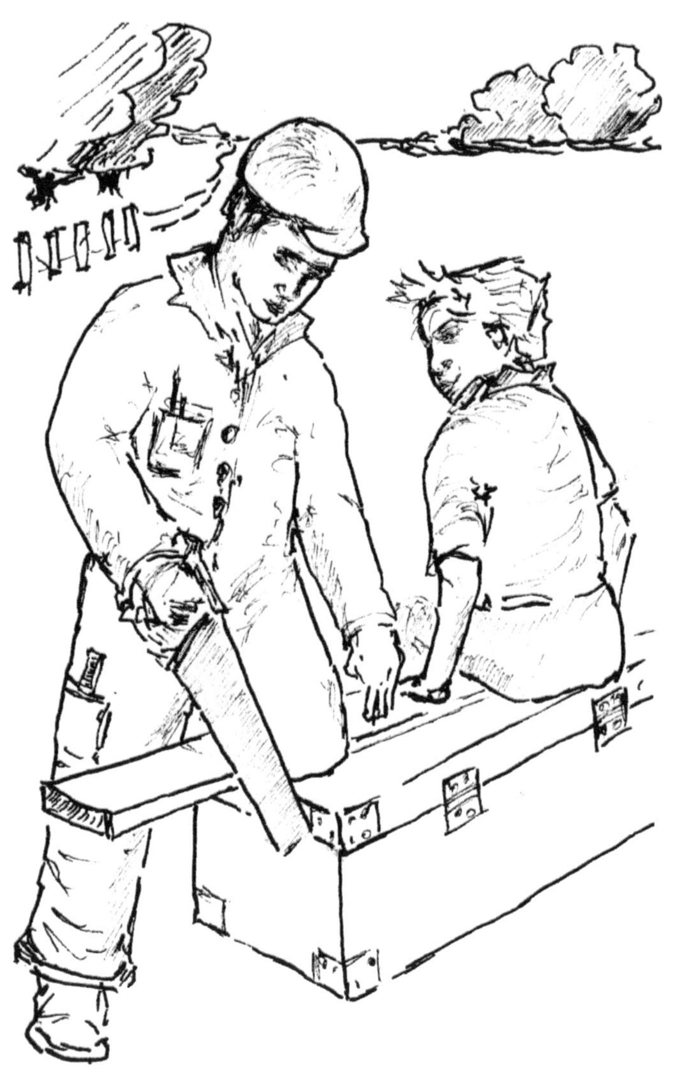

Chapter 10

The Handyman

Farms require an inordinate amount of machinery and equipment to carry out the day to day tasks. Machinery for working the land and the crops, carts, harness, spades and forks of all descriptions, hoes, axes, hedging bills, buildings and barns, milking stools and cow stalls. The list is almost unending. The last item, and the one that only got attention when divorce was threatened, was the farm house or the garden. From time to time all these items required some maintenance or fixing. Hay fork tines were expensive but wooden handles relatively cheap. A fork with a broken handle was never a problem, always supposing you had the tools. We didn't call out the supplier of the machine every time it broke but got down and fixed it.

In my very early youth I learned what the tools were called, what they did, how to look after them and, equally as important, how not to abuse them. Good tools then, and now, are never cheap. It doesn't pay to buy cheap tools anyway. We had a tool shed with everything hung up in its own special place on the wall or on the shelf. Our "tool box" was not a box at all but sacks laid flat with the tools on top, the edges lapped over and then rolled up and secured with a bit of baler twine. There were sacks of tools for wood working and sacks for machinery fixing and building. Crude as this may seem it had several advantages over a proper box. If you were working on a machine in a field of, for example, hay, it was easy to lose the tools in the cut grass. If the sack was opened out, it formed a clean place to put the tools on. Now, with a tool box, how many times have you had to scrabble in the bottom of the box to find the one you want, and it's always at the bottom of the box too? What do you do with all the bigger tools which will always be on the top of the pile? If you are normal, you take them out of the box and put them on the floor. A sure way to lose them in a stack yard covered with chaff at threshing time. Our tools were always counted in and out of the sack, and if there was one missing, you stayed there until it was found. They were always wiped clean and, where required, oiled before they were put back into the toolshed. This early training stood me in very good stead for the future and still, today, my own workshop has a place for everything and everything in its place is the order of the day. Some of my tools still look like new and they must be thirty or forty years old.

It seemed as though there was no job on the farm that was too difficult to tackle. I can clearly remember helping to build some chicken huts. These were very special huts, about eight feet long and five feet wide. They had wooden slatted floors so the droppings could fall through the floor. They were built on wooden railway sleeper bases which were used as skids. They were fitted out with nesting boxes for the hens to lays their eggs in and perches for the hens to sleep on. A lockable door was built and of course the "bob hole", the little opening in the side where the fowls climbed in and out of the hut. The entire hut, full of frightened hens, was dragged by a horse onto fresh grass every second day, early in the morning and before the "bob" was opened. If you did it when the hens were scratching about on the grass, the stupid birds would keep wandering back to where the hut had been previously. It was a very easy matter to hitch up a towing chain onto the hooks on the sleepers and away she went. This meant that we didn't have to clean out the huts and the chicken manure was spread out down the field.

We had a young lad working for us one summer called Harry. 'Arry's aitches were silent, as in 'orse and 'ouse and 'ome. He was about fourteen and hadn't had much to do with farming or animals. One day, he was sent to the field to collect the eggs from the chicken huts. He came scurrying back to the house and burst out with, "Missis, there's an 'en laid a negg in an 'ole in an 'edge an' it's 'atched!"

Making the huts was a fairly slow business as there were always other things to distract us from the job. I was the "fetch me" boy, fetch me a hammer, fetch me a saw and so on. I was the holder down of bits of wood as they were sawn and had to put a spanner on a bolt on the outside as the nut was put on from the inside of the hut. I was allowed to knock in nails and allowed to take them out again when they went in crooked. I was allowed to saw up inconsequential little pieces of wood which we never did anything with, but, at the time, they were important parts of the construction, or so I thought. In these pre-electric days, the wood was sawn by hand and all the holes were drilled into the wood with a brace and bit. The bits had to be meticulously cleaned each evening, oiled, and put back into their special pieces of sack after counting them. I learned some very valuable lessons regarding working with wood. First lesson, measure twice, cut once! Second lesson, measure it again. Always have something heavy at the back if anything is having a nail knocked into it. Never force a saw through wood, let it glide and so on and so on.

We had to have one of our bulls for the dairy herd tied up by his neck against a wall that was about three feet thick. How to secure the bolts holding the chain slide into it? Easy. Chisel a hole in the wall deep enough for the bolts to sit in. Then find all the old lead pipes that had been kept after the frost had split them and melt the lead over a coal fire until it was molten. Pour the lead into the bolt hole in the wall, using a flattened out tin can tacked to the wall to stop it from leaking out. When the lead cooled, you would have needed a bulldozer to pull the bolt out of the wall!

How to throw concrete, how to stick two bricks together, how to mend chains and drive belts, doors, window panes, locks and latches; the list went on and on. Sharpening turnip knives, sickles and scythes until you could shave with them, cleaning the threads on rusty old bolts with diesel fuel, mending burst pipes in winter. Repair the plough, service the tractor and car, make a new canvas table for the binder. Probably the most important thing I learned was not to be afraid of any job. Many people have the ability to do a job but just lack the confidence to make a start on it. Once you start, the job seems to carry itself. Of course, you make mistakes, that is quite permissible. What is not really allowed though, is to make the same mistake twice. That's now verging on being foolish but we all make fools of ourselves at times too.

Nothing was ever thrown away on the farm either. "There'll be a job for that sometime" was always the adage, and eight times out of ten, there always was. To this day I cannot pass a screw, a nail or a washer lying in the street without pocketing it and putting it carefully into a tin in the workshop. And there always seems to be a job for them at some stage! Bits of old timber are kept stacked up against termites and the weather. Bits of steel and old galvanised pipes always come in handy and, do you know anybody who wants an old washing machine pump? I bet it will come in handy one day!

Perhaps one of the most valuable lessons I learned from fixing things is that there are several ways of doing a job. The first thing to do is, consider the options available. If it is something very complicated and specially manufactured like say, a light bulb, then go and buy a new one. With farm machinery and buildings there are many component parts that can be straightened out, cracks welded up, worn shafts fitted with bushes, broken wooded beams spliced together with pieces of wood and some bolts. The art to it is knowing when to buy a new one and when to fix an old one. Sometimes a fixed up one doesn't look as pretty as a new one but the bottom line in black on your bank statement looks prettier than a red one!

Farmers have always had their legs pulled for the clever use of fencing wire and baler twine. Some of the best gates I've seen have been made from barbed wire with wooden droppers tied with baler twine, and the gate latch, a loop of plain wire dropped over the post. Next time you visit a modern farm, just have a close look and I'll bet even money you can still find something fixed with wire or twine!

Chapter 11

Growing Up

Like any other normal lad, I went to primary school, then to Grammar School and did all the exams that were thrown at me, never really excelling in anything other than cross country, rugby 1st team and throwing the javelin, (must have been from the practise throwing hay forks!), but I got by, and was actually a year ahead for my age. I had by now decided that Agriculture, in its broadest sense, was the way forward for me. My parents couldn't afford to send me off to university, something I still regret to this day but now I understand the hardships they were going through. So I elected to go to a local Agricultural College in Yorkshire. One of the entrance qualifications was that the student had to spend a full twelve month period working on an approved farm prior to enrolment. Of course, I did my stint on "The Farm". During this period, we were encouraged to join the local Young Farmers Club which I did, with relish, for several reasons. It was also mandatory that several evenings a week were spent sitting in the local Technical College classrooms.

The Young Farmers Club meetings were held in a local Youth Club Hall and were well attended, not only by pre-college students but by farmer's sons, and more importantly, daughters! There were some real crackers amongst them too, far too good looking really for a young, fit, bunch of hot blooded lads whose hormones were busting out all over!

The major difference between our group and the rest of the youth of the day, I think, was that we had all be brought up with animals and knew that babies were not found under gooseberry bushes, nor were they brought by the stork, but, were the result of a certain action which the boys wanted to take but the girls wouldn't let us!

We had some very good guest speakers on a variety of subjects, not always directly related to agriculture, but on such things as finance and mortgage bonds, lubrication of machinery and how the Stock market worked. We had public speaking competitions and I actually won a very small cup for my account of the "Pallio" in Sienna, Italy, that I had witnessed while on holiday.

There was an annual tractor driving competition which was a lot of fun and a great test of skill. A tractor was hitched to a trailer and three 10 gallon milk churns, all without lids, were filled to the brim with water and placed at the very back of the trailer. The driving course was made into a real obstacle course with humps and mounds in it and some very tight turns too. Fencing stakes lined the sides and, as you went over the humps, care had to be taken not to touch the stakes, especially with the trailer side boards, or that was a penalty. Go too fast and you lost water, too slow and you lost time. You had to drive the course forwards to the half way point where there was a table. There, a sack, filled with straw, was suspended from something that looked like a hangman's scaffold pole so that it was overhanging the table. A beer bottle was placed on the table and the task was to nudge the sack with the nose of the tractor, so delicately, that it knocked the bottle off the table. If the sack hit the pole, it was more penalty points against you. Then reverse back over the course to the starting point. The race was decided by the time each competitor took to cover the course and after deducting any penalty points incurred. Each pint of water it took to fill up the three milk churns to the brims again was also one penalty point. It certainly taught the non farmers how to handle a tractor and was a source of great competition between the farmer's sons, many of who had been born on tractors.

We also had some extremely interesting visits to other farms too. This was the age of very fast technological change in agriculture. Keeping laying hens in battery houses, aerial spraying of crops, irrigation of sugar beet and potatoes, milking parlours. Change was so fast in coming that you had to run to keep up with it.

It was during this time that I purchased my first ever motor car. It was a Hillman Husky, sleek, black and older than it should have been but for £25 it was go-er! It had plenty of attention lavished on it but it still used a fair amount of oil, something that I was reluctant to fix as the fixing would have cost as much as I had paid for the whole car! At least it enabled me to get out and about to the Young Farmers Club meetings and, even more important, to attract the right kind of female company. My heart's desire at that time lived on a farm about fifteen miles away, in a pretty remote spot too. I can remember nearly turning the car over one evening as I was approaching her farm up a narrow road. Vainly, I was looking in the rear view mirror to see if my hair was slicked down well. When I had stopped admiring myself the car was halfway up the off-side grass verge. In a panic, I over corrected and the car shot back to the left hand side of the road, the wheels caught the bank of the grass verge and the whole car tipped over onto its left hand side wheels. It seemed like forever that I did a real film stunt driving on two wheels before the car slammed back onto all four wheels. Arriving at the farm a few minutes later, my heart was still pounding and my teeth still rattling. Her father thought it was because I was nervous of him and the girl thought I was really panting for her.

College itself was a super experience. In those days we had a lot of practical work to do before lectures started. That meant getting up at the crack of dawn or before to milk cows, feed pigs or mess about with chickens. Then it was back to the residence, quick shower, breakfast and lectures for the whole morning. The afternoons were also spent on a lot of practical work too. We had to do a fair amount of the tractor work on the college farm as well as strip and repair machinery in the workshops. I decided that the machinery side was the subject I preferred and so concentrated on that, finishing the course in Agricultural Engineering. Doing that course had ramifications in later life too.

The social side of any tertiary education has got to be balanced to the academic side. We played rugby during the winter season and, until some unfriendly opposition stuck his elbow into my ribs at about 40 miles per hour and cracked one, I enjoyed my game. We also excelled at beer drinking too, to the extent that one of the two local pubs actually banned us from the premises for the rest of the season. We then had to go to the next door village pub which was a bit of a nuisance. Unlike our favourite pub it was just too far to walk to. It was not easy to find somebody who promised to be abstemious enough to be able to drive home a mob of rowdy, schloshed students all piled into one car. On one of these nights, I missed the lift going home and had to walk. I couldn't find the car I think. It was no more than about three miles if you were able to walk down the dark roads in a straight line, which I found was not an easy task that night. When I got back to the college, the gates and doors were locked for the night. No problem, over the fence and shin up the drain pipe, and get my room mate to let me in through the window. He opened the window and

I had to jump and heave my body onto the window sill first and then climb through. I had totally forgotten about the cracked rib and, as my chest made contact with the sharp edge of the window sill, pain shot through my upper body and I let go of the rather tenuous hold that I had. As I lay groaning on the lawn below, one of the masters came by on his nocturnal stroll and caught me. The punishment was to fertilize the two paddocks in front of the college, by hand and over the weekend too! What rotten luck that was as there was an inter college rugby match against our arch rivals, another Agric College, several miles to the east. The rugby was always a needle match but the party afterwards was something else not to be missed. Anyway, my ribs were giving me a lot of pain.

We ate well at the college. All that physical exercise and early morning starts gave us great appetites. The college produced a lot of its own food, milk and cream, eggs and chicken, pork, potatoes and some vegetables from the horticultural section. The milk was stored over night in a large cold room, in cans. The dairy section was only about 400 yards from our residence and we used to take it in turns to sneak up to the dairy with a gallon plastic container. Lovely fresh, ice cold milk was ladled into the container and then sneaked back into the residence. Somebody else would go downstairs into the kitchen and raid the larder there for a couple of loaves of fresh bread and we would feast the night away. This all came to an abrupt temporary halt when one night, we encountered brand new padlocks which had been put onto the cold room door and the entrance to the kitchen. This didn't deter a bunch of hungry young farmers and the next day, we obtained, in good cops and robbers movie style, using a soft candle wax block, the outline of both the keys. The workshop practical was carried out making two spare keys. The authorities must have thought they were mistaken about their stock shrinkage as they never seemed to catch onto the fact. The keys became a very valuable and highly tradable commodity on campus!

As the final year drew to a close, the students were starting to think about their futures and what they would do with their brand new qualifications. One evening, we sat around drinking milk and eating fresh bread onto which we had liberally spread Tate and Lyle Golden Syrup. The latter had happened to "jump" into the bread takers hand from the larder shelf earlier in the evening. Several of the lads were destined for the family farm, others for the commercial world of machinery manufacturers and dealers. Some were joining chemical and fertilizer companies or stock feed mills; a few of us hadn't a clue what to do. I didn't really fancy going back to "The Farm", there was too much happening in the outside world that I hadn't seen, too many places to visit. I had developed a taste for travelling on a four week tour of the Continent with a friend and his family. During that trip I met a young German lad and he came and spent a summer with me on "The Farm". I then had a six week visit to his country, spending three of those weeks at his German school. It was great fun and such an education too.

It was the T & L Golden Syrup tin that gave me inspiration. The well known picture on the tin, if you remember, was a lion with bees buzzing around its dead body and the quotation "Out of the strong came forth sweetness". The lion is surrounded by plants of growing sugar cane. Of course, I had never seen sugar cane except in pictures. "They must need agricultural field staff where they grow this stuff", I said to my pals. "I am going to apply for a job with them". So I sat down and, not knowing who to address the letter to, directed it to Mr Tate of Tate and Lyle. You can imagine my astonishment when a week or so later, a reply came, telling me that they would like to see me for an interview in their London head office. The letter was signed John Tate. They also promised to pay all my travel and out of pocket expenses too which was a good thing because I was pretty broke by then, the pub had most of my allowance. So, off to London I went to meet Mr Tate. He was exceptionally nice to this bumpkin from the North of England. Another strange co-incidence happened too. I mentioned that we had a family friend who had worked in sugar somewhere in the West Indies and who had brought my sister and me sweets during the war. Mr Tate immediately knew him, had done for years and told me all about him, where he worked and what he did. He even gave me an address where my folks could write to him.

Field jobs were available in several parts of the mighty T & L empire. In the West Indies, the estates were long established, well run and the staff had been there for years, I was told. For a young man, it could be a little frustrating as promotion was usually a case of waiting for "dead man's shoes". He then mentioned that they had a new estate, still in the process of being developed, in a place called Chirundu, in Southern Rhodesia. Now I had taken, and passed, geography at school, but if I had been asked to put a mark on an un-named map on Southern Rhodesia, I would have been lucky to have chosen Africa! And, how did you spell "Chirundu" again please? He was quite candid about the place, describing it as a long way from anywhere, sitting on the Zambezi River, hot as hot could be and very little to do except hunt, fish and drink. I couldn't see a lot wrong with that but Mr Tate did say that people didn't tend to settle there very well, so the prospects of quick promotion were very good. The pay he offered me was about twice that which my contemporaries were being offered for jobs in England. So, I took the job.

Ten days after my nineteenth birthday, I was on a B.O.A.C. Comet, a twenty four hour journey, to a place called Salisbury, Southern Rhodesia. I spent a night there in an hotel and the following day took another, smaller, plane, to Lusaka, the capital city of Northern Rhodesia. The mighty Zambezi was the border between Northern and Southern Rhodesia and, Chirundu being right on the river, was actually closer to Lusaka than to Salisbury, hence the round about route. There I was met by a tall, youngish fellow called Glen Eslick, a South African from Natal who was an accountant at the estate. Remember that I was called John in those days. "Are you Richard Shaw" asked Glen calling me by the first name on the bit of paper he had in his hand. "Yes" I replied, too timid to say "No, it's John". So my mother got her way, after nineteen years of waiting to call me by the name she had always wanted to call me. She was delighted, and every letter she wrote, and she wrote regularly every week, without fail, until she died some fifty years later, she addressed me as Richard.

Glen bundled me and my suitcases into his Peugeot 204 car and proceeded to scare the living daylights out of me as we travelled the ninety miles from Lusaka to the estate. The road in those days was narrow eight foot tarmac, full of potholes which Glen avoided with much high speed swerving about. Then we came to the Zambezi Escarpment, a thirty mile nightmare of twists and tight bends as the road dropped from the 4,000 foot highveld to the 1,350 foot Zambezi Valley floor. We saw an ambulance approaching us, dragging its way up the steep hills. Glen said it was the Estate ambulance and promptly stopped it. Inside the ambulance was one of the estate field assistants, the job I was going to take up. He had been badly mauled by a lion on the estate and was being rushed to hospital.

“Welcome to Africa” said Glen with a grin on his face and we continued on to my new life.

Chapter 12

The Re-Visitation

About forty years later, I took my two daughters and wife for a trip down my memory lane. The children had heard many tales but had never visited the place of their father's childhood, his early contact with Mother Nature and the hardships of farming in those days. Now I felt it was time for them to share, if not totally understand, how things were in the "olden days", as they call the time of my youth, rather rudely. But where did this family suddenly spring from? Well, that's another story some other time!

I hadn't been back to "The Farm" for perhaps twenty years. Now remember there were two farms in Carlton, the original and the one that Robert leased from the Coal Board. The leased farm was difficult to find! The road had been re-aligned and the entire farm buildings converted into some very pleasant looking flats and cottages. The old corn chambers, three stories high, were now a row of flats, with windows and doors prettily and gaily painted. The farm yard was grassed in and there was tarmac parking area for cars. The old house had been knocked down altogether and, cleverly re-using the Yorkshire granite stones, a series of new cottages had been built. These cottages extended into the old barn yard too. The paddock, where I had spent many hours playing Cowboys and Indians on the back of an old nag was a housing estate, not as pretty as the cottages and flat, as these were the modern brick and timber ticky-tacky houses as we called them.

The first farm homestead, about half a mile up the road, still looked pretty much the same from the outside, except, the house yard where we had built chicken huts and fixed all sorts of machinery, and kicked a football around in, was now a display area for the flowers and pot plants the new owner sold. I introduced myself and told him the purpose of my visit and would he mind if we had a look around. Rather reluctantly, he agreed and we went into the kitchen. The first thing I did note was that the original AGA cooker was still there! It had a coke fired boiler in my days, it was now oil fired. The kitchen was hardly recognisable otherwise. The huge earthenware sink, big enough to wash a pig carcase in had been replaced with a double stainless steel sink. It was a boxed in affair to match all the other kitchen units.

"You see that wall there" I said to my wife, pointing to one corner section of kitchen units. "That was where the old cupboard was that had a hole in the bottom for the biscuit tins of money".

The new owner looked at me very peculiarly and I could almost see his mind turning over like a cart wheel. Buried treasure? I hope he didn't rip out his super kitchen fittings because the cupboard would certainly have been bare!

The big Yorkshire Stone floor flags were not visible as the floor was covered with some sort of vinyl roll floor covering. I bet that was a blessing to them as the old floor was as cold as charity in the winter. They had obviously, and very tastefully, spent thousands of pounds on the renovations. Central heating was evident too and the windows double glazed. We were not invited to go further than the kitchen so I can't comment on the rest of the house, but I would have paid to go through it. We had, in the olden days, an outside toilet; actually, it was a long drop. The remarkable thing about this loo was that it was a very sociable one. It had two holes cut into the timber, each protected by a covering piece of timber with a handle on it. The holes were rather big and I can remember having to hang on to the sides for dear life or fall into the midden below. Although no longer in use, at least the old place had been left standing, or sitting, depending on how you view these things. The family sniggered, the youngest daughter, was wide eyed and just said, "Dad??? Uuuurgh"!

The new owner was essentially a market gardener, growing pot and bedding plants, shrubs and roses for the millions of houses now in the area. He said he only had fifteen acres of land left which he grew his plants on. The rest of the land had been used for industrial or residential building.

We went down to see the old cattle mistle, barns, sheds and the rest. They were now small industrial premises; I saw a workshop, with lathes and a milling machine visible through one open door and a joinery workshop through another. The old corn chamber had been converted into offices; a computer firm were advertising their whereabouts on one door and a firm of accountants on another. The old stone steps that the spring lambs had climbed up had been demolished and replaced with a functional wrought iron set. It didn't look like a farm yard at all. Nonplussed, I told the family we would go and look at their great grandfather's property on Willy Row. It wasn't there. In its place was an enormous Marks and Spencer warehouse. The old colliery had closed years before and was a rusting, dilapidated mess of old pit head winding gear and dirty looking, broken windowed buildings. The fields at the back of the warehouse, (good crops of corn came off there), were now covered with more houses. Where had all the people come from? They couldn't have done this to all of the area, I thought, as we piled back into the car. We went to find the woodlands area that had been cleared during the war by the Land Girls. I could remember the way, or so I thought. The old cart track we used was now a wide major road, traffic lights and all on it. Most confusing, and then suddenly, I recognised something! An old oak tree that had been responsible for catching the tops of many a cart load of corn. It had to be the same tree, as oaks that size don't grow in forty years. It was now sitting in the front garden of somebody's house plot.

To say the least, I was shattered. My children were getting very restless and bored by now, they had come to see their father's roots and all they had been shown to date were housing and industrial estates; what a let down for them. It's almost impossible to engender enthusiasm from a third party by saying, you see that place there, well, that was where we once built a hay stack that caught fire. All they could see was a small supermarket. We did find something that hadn't changed a bit from the look of it. The old church, which was compulsorily attended every Sunday evening, was still there. My grand father and my father had both sung in the choir at this church too. We couldn't get in because it had a fairly new set of high gates on it that were securely padlocked. Not the little lych gate that had been there in my day, where the vicar used to stand under the tiled roof to bid us all welcome. The large notice board which used to have all the service times on it, now read "Carlton Parish Hall. Bingo five nights a week". Even the church had gone. What a Godless lot, I thought.

"Never mind", said I to the family, "I'll take you to where I was born in the next village", and we motored on.

"You see this railway line", I said as we clacked across it.

"That used to carry coal from the colliery to the canal down there". We used to fish in the canal as boys until it became too expensive on tackle and dangerous with old bicycle and perambulator frames thrown in it. We actually stopped swimming in it the day we found a sack full of drowned puppies floating on the water. We motored on.

Glory be! The house that I had entered the world in was still there! Now I had something to show. Very politely I knocked on the door of the house. The door was flung open by a middle aged man in his shirt sleeves.

"What does tha want", he aggressively said. I explained that I had been born in his house and had brought my family all this way, many thousands of miles, to see it. Would it be possible for them to have just a little peek inside?

"No, tha bloody well can't", he said and slammed the door in my face.

I had saved my moment of final glory until last. My maternal grandfather had been the manager of another coal mine and lived in the only white painted house in the village, down the road from where I had been born. It was a local landmark, being possibly the biggest house in the village in it's day. We arrived at the gate which had a sign outside it advertising that it was the head office of a security company.

"Well", I remarked, "at least we might get a better reception here", and marched into the front office. The young receptionist was painting her fingernails a bright red colour to match her dyed hair. I asked to see the person in charge to be told he was away on holiday. Then the next person in charge please. He's gone out and won't be back for a few hours. Oh dear, I explained that the house had belonged to my grandfather and please could I bring my family in to have a look around?

"Sorry", she said without pausing with her finger painting exercise, "It's against cumpany policy, we are a security cumpany yer know", she added without looking at me at all.

"And I'm 'ere on me own", she added, her tone of voice indicating, I am the sergeant and I'm in charge, now bugger off.

I left the office, it had been the dining room too, and told the now thoroughly bored family that we couldn't get in. All day I had been thwarted at every turn to try to show my family a bit of my history. Our youngest daughter, about twelve then said, "Dad, are you sure all the stories you told us about farming are true or did you just make them all up?"

I'll leave you to be the judge of that.

The End

www.ingramcontent.com/pod-product-compliance
Ingram Content Group UK Ltd.
Pitfield, Milton Keynes, MK11 3LW, UK
UKHW040015200726
13854UKWH00001B/208

9 781456 776282